Meeting
College Costs

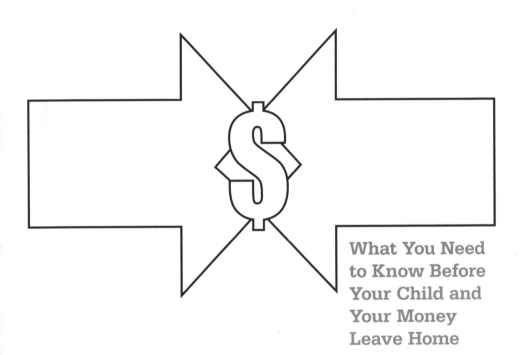

What You Need
to Know Before
Your Child and
Your Money
Leave Home

Meeting
College Costs

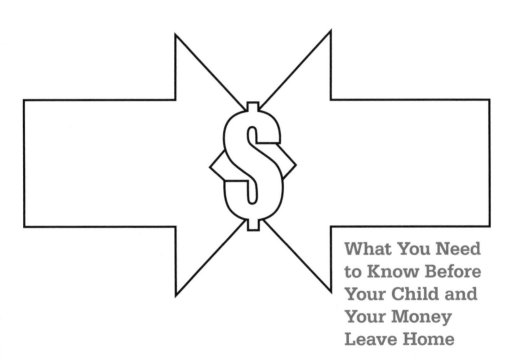

**What You Need
to Know Before
Your Child and
Your Money
Leave Home**

A workbook for families

The College Board: Connecting Students to College Success

The College Board is a not-for-profit membership association whose mission is to connect students to college success and opportunity. Founded in 1900, the association is composed of more than 5,200 schools, colleges, universities, and other educational organizations. Each year, the College Board serves seven million students and their parents, 23,000 high schools, and 3,500 colleges through major programs and services in college admissions, guidance, assessment, financial aid, enrollment, and teaching and learning. Among its best-known programs are the SAT®, the PSAT/NMSQT®, and the Advanced Placement Program® (AP®). The College Board is committed to the principles of excellence and equity, and that commitment is embodied in all of its programs, services, activities, and concerns. For further information, visit www.collegeboard.com.

Printed in the United States of America.

Contents

Whose Obligation Is This, Anyway?

If you are like most parents who face the prospect of a child going off to college, you are excited about the opportunities that lie ahead—and filled with trepidation about how you will afford those opportunities and still have a life (not to mention a retirement) of your own. You have probably read about or heard about the cost of college today. And you are probably aware that for most families, providing a college education for their children is the largest investment (other than buying their home) that they will make.

Some families are convinced that they will get no help and will have to pay the total costs from current income and savings. Others believe that the costs of a college education should be shouldered by the government, the college, and the student. These families are neither completely right nor totally wrong.

The Financing Partnership

While it may be obvious that the student will benefit most from the college experience, others will benefit as well.

➡ You, the **parents**, will benefit through exposure to new ideas and the enjoyment from watching your child gain skills that lead to independence.

➡ The **country** will gain as your child moves into the world of work and becomes a taxpayer.

➡ **Employers** will gain another member of the trained workforce.

➡ **Colleges** will gain by increasing the group of loyal alumni who will support the institution in future years.

Just as buying your home involved a partnership—your investment, perhaps some family help, a mortgage lender—this major investment in a college education will likely involve a partnership as well. To some degree, unless you are extremely wealthy (and therefore probably not reading this book!), several of these partners may share in the financing of your child's education.

Most colleges will presume, however, that the primary responsibility for meeting college costs falls to parents. Over the months prior to your child's entering college, you will be asked to provide information about your financial circumstances so that federal and state governments, as well as the colleges to which your child is applying, can determine how much of the cost of education you will be able to pay. Your child's savings and income will also be taken into account. As you will learn later in this book, there are standardized methods of determining your family's expected share of the costs, but many colleges will try to be sensitive to your family's particular financial situation.

You will find that the other college financing partners offer a variety of options if college costs are beyond your financial ability.

➡ Your child may qualify for **grant money** (gift money that does not have to be repaid) from the federal government or your own state government, and/or from the college your child will attend. While some college-sponsored grants are awarded strictly on the basis of merit, most are offered based on financial need or a combination of need and merit.

➡ You and your child may also qualify for **low-interest loans** with favorable terms (for example, no payments due until after the student graduates from college). (See pages 87–89.)

➡ Some businesses and civic organizations offer **scholarship money** to students who meet their selection criteria.

➡ And there are increasing numbers of **opportunities** for families whose expected contribution *would* cover the cost of college **to borrow money** so that college payments can be spread over a longer time period. (See pages 87–89.)

How This Book Can Help

Meeting College Costs will give you the information you need to make the most of this partnership. You will learn:

➡ how to determine what the costs really are for each of the colleges your child is considering

➡ what types of financial aid are available

➡ how the government and the colleges will determine your eligibility for financial aid

➡ how divorced or separated parents may be evaluated for financial aid

➡ which financial aid forms to complete, and when

➡ how to interpret the financial aid offers your child receives

➡ what to do if the financial aid you receive is not enough

➡ why most families find that college is worth the cost

➡ how your high-school-age child fits into the college financing partnership

➡ how your child can manage his or her finances during college

Throughout the book you will find special tips, charts, tables, and case studies to which you can compare your own situation, and worksheets to help you make your way through the process as an informed consumer. We will also attempt to dispel some of the myths surrounding the financial aid process; and we'll provide definitions of the financial aid terms and acronyms most commonly used. Look for the following symbols in each chapter:

 Important **tips** from the College Board

 Myths—why commonly held beliefs aren't necessarily true

 Additional **resources** for more information on a subject

 Questions parents should ask colleges to become informed consumers

 Helpful **worksheets** to help you prepare for the financial aid process

There are topics you won't find addressed in this book, such as the intricacies of rearranging one's financial situation in an effort to qualify for more aid, or details about the financial aid policies of particular colleges. We will, however, provide suggestions for other resources should you want more information.

Our first piece of advice? DON'T PANIC! By reading this book, you are on the way to understanding how you can send your child to a college that he or she will find compatible academically and socially, and that you as a family can afford.

Throughout the book you will find questions to ask the colleges to which your child is applying and worksheets to complete. If you do your homework, you'll be well prepared to help your child make a good college choice.

How Much Will College REALLY Cost?

The first step in your planning process is to understand what the total costs will be at each of the colleges your child is considering. It might seem that defining costs should be relatively straightforward. In many cases, though, you will find that it is not. While information about "billable" costs (tuition, student fees, room and board) is readily available in each college's literature, you also need to be aware of other expenses that may have a substantial impact on total college costs.

Most colleges provide information for an average student's cost of attendance that includes tuition, student fees, and room and board, as well as estimated expenses for books and supplies, personal expenses, and transportation to and from campus. Let's look at these components and some of the factors, hidden and otherwise, that could impact the total college cost.

Cost Components

Tuition

Tuition is one of the most easily defined components in the student budget. For most colleges there is a published cost for tuition per academic term. But some colleges link tuition to the number of credit hours the student takes, and other colleges charge tuition based on level of enrollment (part-time, full-time). In any case, it should be fairly easy to estimate annual tuition.

Consider strategies to reduce costs, such as shortening the time it takes to graduate by bringing in Advanced Placement Program® (AP®) credit or taking summer classes at a community college. Don't rule out a college solely on the basis of high tuition!

Fees

When fees are listed as a billable cost, they refer to the charges assessed every student to help pay for the necessary extras of campus life, usually in the student activity area. These fees help subsidize the cost of activities, such as concerts, lectures, and athletic events, so that most students will be able to attend events without large out-of-pocket expenses. The student activity fee is usually the same for everyone and should be clearly stated in the college cost literature. Some fees that do require detective work are outlined below under "Other Costs."

Room and Board

There is variation in how colleges define room and board costs. Some have a set, billable cost for room and board, covering any room on campus and a one-size-fits-all meal plan. But others have a graduated scale of payment for housing, based on the assessed "quality" of the living arrangement (single rooms often cost more, for example). You'll need to get a sense of the range of housing costs like these to put together a reasonable budget; the amount appearing in the cost-of-attendance budget is usually for the "average" room (in most cases a double in a typical residence hall). For schools offering meal plan options, be realistic about what your child will likely need; students who don't get up in time for breakfast should find a plan that covers only the other two meals of the day.

We can save a lot of money by having our child live at home during college.

While it is almost certain to cost less to have your child live at home rather than on campus, don't forget students who live at home cost money, too! In addition to the food and utilities they consume at home, there will be the inevitable pick-up meals on campus. Among the big costs commuters must cover are car insurance and maintenance, gas, and parking fees, or the cost of public transportation. Unless it is essential to have your child live at home, be sure to consider the pluses of living on campus that are *not* quantifiable in terms of cost: more opportunities for your child to socialize and become involved in campus life, and the opportunity to mature and become independent more quickly.

Books and Supplies

College viewbooks generally provide an estimate of what a typical student can expect to spend on books and supplies. Until your child is on campus and determines exactly which books and supplies are required in the courses he or she is taking, however, it is difficult to know where adjustments may need to be made in the estimate. Students majoring in English or history may find the estimate fairly accurate. Those majoring in biology or architecture may not.

It's best to find out what you can about variations in book expenses before enrollment, and plan to be economical if need be. A used book may be a better value than a new book, and at most colleges these are readily available.

Personal Expenses

As you might imagine, this is an area where the student's lifestyle can make a major difference in the cost. Colleges provide an estimate of what it is likely to cost a typical student to do laundry, go to campus events, order an occasional pizza, and the like. However, a penchant for late-night junk food, an insatiable need to see first-run movies, or a habit of long-distance calls to a friend can add up.

Transportation

It's essential to find out what a college considers in making an estimate of your child's travel expenses. For example, some residential colleges build into the total budget an allowance for two roundtrips between home and college per year; others budget one or three. Depending on the distance home, car or air travel costs will be estimated. For colleges where students commute, some estimate will be made for commuting costs. You'll want to know what factors are considered in putting together the estimate (gas, parking, insurance, number of trips weekly) and determine as best you can how your child's actual experience may vary.

Other Costs

If all these costs weren't complicated enough, there are other, less obvious costs to consider.

➡ There may be special lab fees for some of the science courses your child plans to take, or drop-and-add fees for changing a course schedule.

➡ Some colleges require all students, or those planning to major in certain fields, to purchase a computer. The cost of the computer may be included in the cost of education at some of these colleges.

➡ Many colleges charge students for health insurance. In most cases, these fees may be waived if the student is covered by health insurance with the parent. If your child has unusually high medical costs, consider those in making your plans.

➡ If your child is committed to decorating a residence hall room with posters, there may be a fee assessed at the end of the year to repair the walls.

➡ And, if your child decides to participate in such activities as athletics, music, or a sorority or fraternity, there will be additional costs.

You may be able to find out about some of these costs in advance. In any event, you should plan on some miscellaneous additional costs beyond those addressed in the standard cost-of-attendance budget.

 Keep track of the costs at the colleges your child is considering by completing the worksheet at the end of this chapter.

2007-08 Academic Year Undergraduate Student Budgets

The following table displays average student charges and expenses for colleges responding to the College Board's most recent *Annual Survey of Colleges*. The sample budgets are illustrative of the kinds of fixed charges and additional expenses that students and their families faced during the 2007-08 academic year.* (These costs will most likely increase for the next academic year.) "Resident" budgets represent expenses for students living on campus; "commuter" budgets illustrate costs that students who live at home will incur.

College Sector	Tuition and Fees	Books and Supplies	Room and Board	Transportation	Other Personal Expenses	Total Expenses
2-year public						
Commuter	$2,385	$890	$6,615**	$1,250	$1,760	$12,900
4-year public						
Resident	6,140	985	7,325	925	1,775	17,150
Commuter	6,140	985	7,240**	1,285	2,150	17,800
4-year private						
Resident	23,330	985	8,560	760	1,340	34,975
Commuter	23,330	985	7,570**	1,150	1,715	34,750

* These average costs are based on the College Board's 2006–2007 *Annual Survey of Colleges* and are inflated by 5 percent to arrive at estimated 2007–2008 costs.

** Room and board expenses for commuter students represent living expenses for students living off campus but not with parents.

Meet the Smith, the Washington, and the Martinez Families

We will follow three representative students and their families as they move through the financial aid application and award and college selection processes. You may compare these families and their experiences to your own.

Sarah Smith

Sarah expects to graduate near the top of her public high school class in June 2008 and major in English at college.

Sarah's parents are divorced. She lives with her mother, who manages a small insurance office, and two younger brothers, ages 15 and 12. The family rents an apartment in downtown Chicago.

Sarah's father is a teacher. As you'll see later, although her father no longer lives with the family, one of Sarah's college options will collect financial information from him and will expect him to help pay for her educational expenses.

Sarah is considering three colleges: Prairie (a four-year public university within commuting distance of home), Old Bricks (a four-year private college in the Midwest), and Central (another four-year private college in the South). After some research, she and her mother determined the following costs for each:

	Prairie	**Old Bricks**	**Central**
Tuition and Fees	$7,425	$21,800	$20,200
Room and Board	(board only) 3,350	7,000	7,400
Books and Supplies	850	1,000	950
Personal Expenses	1,950	1,425	1,425
Transportation	825	775	1,025
TOTAL	$14,400	$32,000	$31,000

James Washington

James will graduate from a private preparatory school in Boston in June 2008. He is an above-average student and hopes to major in engineering at college.

James lives with both his parents. His father works in sales and his mother is an active volunteer in the community. James has a younger sister, age 13, who also lives at home.

The family has unusually high medical expenses as a result of a long-term illness suffered by James's sister. The parents own their home.

James is considering three colleges: Colony (a four-year public university in Boston), Very Old Bricks (a four-year private college), and Division (another four-year private college located within commuting distance). James and his parents determined the following costs for each:

	Colony	Very Old Bricks	Division
Tuition and Fees	$10,100	$36,400	$28,400
Room and Board	7,200	10,100	(board only) 5,800
Books and Supplies	1,275	975	625
Personal Expenses	725	1,000	1,075
Transportation	600	625	1,300
TOTAL	$19,900	$49,100	$37,200

Maria Martinez

Maria grew up in Phoenix, Arizona, and will graduate from high school there in June 2008. A good student and a highly ranked tennis player, Maria plans to major in biology and pursue premedical studies in college.

Maria lives with her parents. Her mother is a dentist and her father is a real estate developer. The family includes six children: Maria, an older brother who is a college junior, and four younger children, ages 16, 14, 13, and 10. The parents are homeowners.

Maria is also considering three colleges: Canyon (a two-year public college in Phoenix), Major Mortar (a four-year private college in California), and Midway (another four-year private college in the Midwest). Maria and her parents, after research, determined the following costs for each:

	Canyon	**Major Mortar**	**Midway**
Tuition and Fees	$1,800	$34,400	$22,800
Room and Board	(board only) 3,975	8,400	7,300
Books and Supplies	800	1,200	1,000
Personal Expenses	1,575	1,850	1,250
Transportation	1,350	750	950
TOTAL	$9,530	$46,600	$33,300

My child shouldn't even consider her first-choice college if it costs too much.

It's true that the total expenses for some colleges are lower than those for others. As you'll see when you fill in the College Costs worksheet at the end of this chapter, this is largely due to the difference in the cost of tuition. Tuition is subsidized at public colleges by taxpayers and is usually less at two-year public colleges than at four-year public colleges or universities. There's usually not a lot of difference in the other costs. You should also keep in mind that private colleges often have more financial aid, and more flexibility in awarding it, to help make up the difference between their costs and what your family can afford.

According to *Trends in College Pricing and Student Aid 2006*, almost 62 percent of full-time undergraduate students receive grant aid. And millions of students and parents benefit from federal education tax credits or tuition and fee deductions. As a result, for the majority of students, the actual price of college is lower than the published price.*

As you'll see in Chapter 4, the greater your overall college expenses, the greater the possibility of demonstrating eligibility for financial aid.

*For more information, see *Trends in College Pricing* at http://www.collegeboard.com/prof/index.html.

For more information on college costs:

College admissions and financial aid offices

College and university Web sites on the Internet

College Board on the Web: www.collegeboard.com

The *Guide to Getting Financial Aid 2008*. This how-to reference for students and parents outlines major aid programs, discusses how financial aid is determined, and lists current costs and scholarship opportunities at 3,000 two- and four-year public, private, and proprietary institutions. Revised annually. Available in bookstores and in libraries.

 Questions Families Should Ask About College Costs

You can find answers to these questions by reviewing college viewbooks and talking to admissions and/or financial aid administrators at the colleges your child is considering.

1. Does the college charge a standard amount for tuition and fees for the academic year, or does tuition vary by enrollment status (number of credits carried)? If tuition varies, what is the typical number of credits carried by first-year students? Upperclass students?

2. Does the college give academic credit for AP courses? Under what conditions?

3. Does the cost of a residence hall room vary by the quality of the room or other factors? What is the cost of a single room? A double room? A triple room?

4. Are first-year students permitted to live off campus? What is the range of rental costs in the area of the campus?

5. Are there meal plan options? What meals are covered by the standard meal plan?

6. What are the typical costs for books and supplies for our child's intended major?

7. Are all students expected to own computers, or only students in certain majors? Are computers readily available in computer labs?

8. How much should we budget for our child's personal expenses? What types of expenses does this take into account?

9. Does the financial aid office take into account transportation home? How many round-trips per year? Is it assumed that our child will be flying or driving?

10. Are there special fees to consider?
    • lab fees?
    • health insurance? (Is this mandatory?)
    • music?
    • sorority/fraternity?
    • athletics?
    • loan fees?

11. How long will it take my child to graduate? What percentage of the college's students graduate in four years? Five years? More than five years? Does the graduation rate vary by major?

12. What is the *total cost* of education for the average undergraduate student?

13. By what percentage have costs increased each year for the past five years?

Worksheet 1:
Comparing College Costs

College Name	1.	2.	3.	4.
Tuition				
Billable Fees				
Room Costs				
Board Costs				
Books/Supplies				
Personal Costs				
Transportation				
Other Costs				
TOTAL COSTS				

**What Types of Financial Aid Are Available?**

Now that you have a sense of the college costs you'll be facing, you are undoubtedly wondering where you might get help in meeting them. You'll find below a quick description of the major sources of financial aid available to families. Other private sources include:

➡ benefits offered by your employer

➡ competitive scholarships available from civic or religious groups

➡ scholarships targeted to students pursuing specific majors

If you'd like to know more about those types of opportunities, check with your child's school counselor, or follow up on some of the suggested resources at the end of the chapter.

 Millions of scholarship dollars go unused every year.

If you're aware of this myth, you probably heard it from a representative of a scholarship search service. That's because they'd like you to pay them to look

for these scholarships for you. The claim that millions go unused has never been verified. With the advice you're finding in this book, you should be able to find, without a professional search service, the money for which your child is eligible.

Three general categories of financial aid are awarded to undergraduate college students. Most students qualifying for aid will receive a combination of "gift" and "self-help" funding.

➡ **Grants and Scholarships** are funds awarded to students without expectation of repayment (sometimes referred to as "gift" aid). Sources of grants include federal and state governments, colleges, and private organizations.

➡ **Loans** are borrowed by students and parents to help meet college costs and must be repaid with interest. This "self-help" aid is available through the federal and state governments, institutions, and private lenders. The terms of some loans are more favorable than others, as you will see later in this chapter.

➡ **Student Employment.** The Federal Work-Study program is the best known of these "self-help" programs, where students work either on or off campus for an hourly salary. Some colleges have other student employment options either on or off campus.

Financial Aid Available Through the Federal Government

The federal government is the largest single source of financial assistance for students and families. You and your child apply for this assistance by completing the Free Application for Federal Student Aid (FAFSA); you'll find more about that in Chapters 4 and 5.

Grants
Federal Pell Grants

This is the government's largest need-based student aid program. Pell Grants range from a minimum of $400 to a maximum of $4,310 for 2007–2008. (It is possible that the maximum award will increase in 2008–2009.) The size of the grant a student receives is based on the family's financial need, the cost of education at the college the student attends, the length of the program in which he or she is enrolled, and whether enrollment is full- or part-time.

Congress recently enacted the Higher Education Reconciliation Act of 2005 that created two new federal grants for Pell Grant recipients who meet the eligibility requirements. However, unlike other sources of federal aid, these grants are available for U.S. citizens only; permanent residents are not eligible for these additional grant funds.

➡ **The Academic Competitiveness Grant** provides an additional $750 for students during their first year of study and $1,300 for their second year, provided the student meets the following eligibility criteria:

- U.S. citizens who are also Pell Grant recipients
- Enrolled full-time in a degree program
- Have completed a "rigorous secondary school program of study" (More information about this qualification can be found at http://studentaid.ed.gov/PORTALSWebApp/students/english/NewPrograms.jsp.)
- Maintain a 3.0 GPA in order to qualify for the second year ACG of $1,300

➡ **The National SMART Grant (National Science and Mathematics ACCESS to RETAIN Talent Grant)** provides an additional $4,000 annually to Pell Grant recipients who meet the following eligibility requirements:

- U.S. citizens who are enrolled full-time in a four-year degree-granting program
- Are enrolled in an eligible major in physical science, life science, computer science, engineering, mathematics, technology, or a critical foreign language
- Have earned a minimum cumulative 3.0 GPA (on a 4.0 scale) in their major course work. (More information about this grant can be found at the Web site listed above.)

Federal Supplemental Educational Opportunity Grants

Otherwise known as SEOG, these grants are campus based, meaning that while the money comes from the federal government, the colleges are in charge of distributing the money to students who have financial need. Recipients must be enrolled in an undergraduate program at an accredited college or university. Grants of up to $4,000 a year are awarded on the basis of need.

Work-Study
Federal Work-Study Program (FWS)

This is a campus-based federal program providing employment opportunities for students who are enrolled at the undergraduate or graduate level. Students are usually employed on campus, though off-campus jobs can be arranged and are quite popular at some colleges. Students are generally paid at least the prevailing federal minimum wage. Although students can work as many hours a week as their award will support, 10 to 15 hours is typical for first-year students. FWS eligibility is based on the student's demonstrated financial need.

Campus-Based Loans
Federal Perkins Loans

Perkins Loans are campus based and administered by colleges and universities. They carry the lowest interest rate of any educational loans (5 percent), and repayment is deferred until a student graduates or leaves school. Students may be eligible to borrow up to $4,000 for each year of undergraduate study. The amount will depend on the funds available at the school. Nine months after a student leaves school, regular payments are required over a maximum period of 10 years until the total amount, including interest, is repaid. Repayment can sometimes be further deferred for service in the military, the Peace Corps, or approved comparable organizations.

Federal Loan Programs

Borrowers must be enrolled in college as at least half-time students. Freshmen may borrow up to $3,500 for the first year, and upperclassmen may borrow more, up to a maximum of $4,500 a year for dependent undergraduates who have completed their first year of study, and up to $5,500 a year for students who have completed two years of study. Under certain circumstances (at least half-time study, approved graduate fellowship programs, or economic hardship), repayment may be deferred temporarily. The repayment schedule is worked out between the student and the lender.

Subsidized Federal Stafford Loans

These loans permit students with demonstrated need to borrow money for educational expenses from private sources (such as banks, credit unions, savings and loan associations, and educational organizations) at interest rates lower than most commercially available loans. The federal government pays the interest while the student is enrolled. Repayment is deferred until six months after a student graduates or leaves school. The maximum interest rate is 8.25 percent.

Unsubsidized Federal Stafford Loans

These loans are intended for use by students who do not qualify for a subsidized Stafford Loan and/or who need additional funds. The amounts, interest rates, and terms are the same as for the subsidized loans, with important differences: repayment begins as soon as the loan is disbursed; or, if the borrower opts to begin repayment after leaving school, interest charges are assessed from the time the loan is disbursed and will accrue during the in-school period.

Federal Direct Loan Program (FDLP)

Students at some postsecondary institutions can borrow subsidized and unsubsidized Federal Direct Loans through this program, which is administered at the college. If the college your child attends is participating in FDLP, the financial aid office will tell you more about these loans. The conditions are the same as for Stafford Loans; however, the lender is the federal government.

Preliminary Projected Monthly Payment, Federal Stafford Program

Amount Borrowed	Number of Payments	Estimated Monthly Payments	Recommended Annual Salary
$ 4,000	107	$ 50*	$ 7,500
$ 8,000	120	$ 92	$ 13,800
$ 13,000	120	$ 150	$ 22,400
$ 18,000	120	$ 207	$ 31,100
$ 23,000	120	$ 265	$ 39,700
$ 33,000	120	$ 380	$ 57,900
$ 43,000	120	$ 495	$ 74,200
$ 53,000	120	$ 610	$ 91,500
$ 63,000	120	$ 725	$108,800
$ 73,000	120	$ 840	$126,000

Recommended annual figures are based on 8 percent of income available for student loan repayment. Generally, manageable student loan payments range between 5 and 15 percent of income. Examples of average salaries follow on page 26.

* Minimum payment of $50.

For Stafford Loans first disbursed beginning July 1, 2006, the interest rate is fixed at 6.8 percent.

Federal PLUS Loans

PLUS Loans are available to parents of eligible students and graduate students to assist in financing college costs. These loans are not need based. Parents and graduate students can borrow up to the total cost of education minus any financial aid received each year. To qualify for a PLUS Loan, a borrower cannot have an adverse credit history.

Preliminary Projected Monthly Payment, Federal PLUS Program

Amount Borrowed	Number of Payments	Estimated Monthly Payments	Recommended Annual Salary
$ 4,000	119	$ 50*	$ 7,500
$ 8,000	120	$ 99	$ 14,900
$ 13,000	120	$ 161	$ 24,200
$ 18,000	120	$ 223	$ 33,500
$ 23,000	120	$ 285	$ 42,800
$ 33,000	120	$ 409	$ 61,400
$ 43,000	120	$ 533	$ 80,000
$ 53,000	120	$ 657	$ 98,600
$ 63,000	120	$ 781	$ 117,200
$ 73,000	120	$ 905	$ 135,800

Recommended annual figures are based on 8 percent of income available for loan repayment. Generally, manageable loan payments range between 5 and 15 percent of income.

* Minimum payment of $50.

The interest rate for Plus Loans first disbursed on or after July 1, 2006, is fixed at 8.5 percent.

Estimated Annual Salaries

Listed below are the average annual salaries for a variety of careers. Keep in mind that these are averages, and many in each occupation earn more or less. For more information on salaries, please consult the latest edition of the *Occupational Outlook Handbook* at your library or view the online version at http://www.bls.gov/oco/.

Up to $29,999

Bank Teller	$21,100	Nursing Aide	$21,000
Child Care Worker	18,800	Receptionist	21,800
Data Entry Keyer	28,000	Travel Agent	27,600
Dental Assistant	28,300		

$30,000 to $49,999

Civil Engineer	$43,700	Librarian	45,900
Computer Operator	31,100	Machinist	33,900
Dietician	43,600	Paralegal	39,100
Flight Attendant	43,400	Personnel Clerk	31,700
Food Service Manager	39,600	Teacher	45,500
Graphic Designer	38,000	Television Reporter	37,800

$50,000 to $74,999

Accountant	$51,000	Medical Scientist	61,300
Aerospace Engineer	51,000	Nurse	52,300
Architect	60,300	Occupational Therapist	54,600
Chemist	56,100	School Psychologist	54,900
Environmental Scientist	51,500	Statistician	58,600
Landscape Architect	53,100	Veterinarian	66,500
Management Analyst	63,400		

$75,000 and Over

Academic Dean of Business	$120,000	Information Systems Manager	$92,570
Attorney	94,900	Optometrist	88,400
Computer Engineer	75,000	Pharmacist	84,900
Dentist	129,900	Psychiatrist	174,000
Federal District Judge	162,000	Physician	142,000

Source: *Occupational Outlook Handbook*, 2006–07 Edition, http://www.bls.gov/oco/

For more information about careers and projected annual salaries, visit www.collegeboard.com/myroad.

Education Tax Credits

Taxpayers may qualify for education tax credits, which are designed to make a college education more affordable for families with moderate incomes. Tax credits reduce the amount of federal income tax a family owes. There are two types of tax credits:

⇒ **Hope Tax Credit.** A family may claim a tax credit of up to $1,650 per year for each eligible family member enrolled at least half-time in the first two years of undergraduate study. The student must be claimed as a dependent by the taxpayer claiming the credit. The amount of the credit depends in part on the family's income—the credit is phased out for single taxpayers with incomes between $45,000 and $55,000 and for married taxpayers with incomes between $90,000 and $110,000. The amount of the credit is also based on the qualified tuition and fee expenses paid by the taxpayer.

⇒ **Lifetime Learning Tax Credit.** A family may claim a tax credit of 20 percent of tuition and fees, up to a maximum of $2,000 per year for all eligible family members. (This is a per-family maximum, not a per-student maximum.) To be eligible, the student must be claimed by the taxpayer, and must be taking courses at an eligible school, but does not necessarily have to be enrolled in a degree program or enrolled half-time. As with the Hope credit, the Lifetime Learning credit is phased out at the income levels defined above.

Financial Aid Available Through States

Every state has a program to provide some form of need-based financial assistance to eligible students who are legal residents of the state. Some states also have funds available to students who meet specific eligibility requirements, regardless of need (for example, based on outstanding academic ability or program of study). Most of these aid funds are stipulated for use at colleges and universities within the state, although a few are "portable" (students can use the funds when attending a college in another state that has a reciprocal agreement with the home state). You'll want to check with your child's school counselor or the financial aid office at a local college, or contact your state education agency for information about what programs are available in your state and how to apply for them. Deadlines for applying for 2008-09 are listed on page 29. If your state is not listed, contact the agency directly. Or visit www.ed.gov for links to all state scholarship program information.

State Aid Deadlines

State	Deadline	Explanation of Deadline
Alaska	April 15, 2008	Date application received
Arkansas	June 1, 2008	Date application received
Arizona	June 30, 2009	Date application received
California*†	March 2, 2008 (initial awards)	Date application received
	September 2, 2008	Date application postmarked
	(for additional community college awards)	
Delaware	April 15, 2008	Date application received
District of Columbia*	June 30, 2008	Date application received
Florida	May 15, 2008	Date application processed
Illinois#	September 30, 2008	First-time applicants
	August 15, 2008	Continuing applicants (date received)
Indiana	March 10, 2008	Date application received
Iowa†	July 1, 2008	Date application received
Kansas*#	April 1, 2008	Date application received
Kentucky#	March 15, 2008	Date application received
Louisiana†#	May 1, 2008	Date application received
	July 1, 2008 (final deadline)	
Maine	May 1, 2008	Date application received
Maryland	March 1, 2008	Date application received
Massachusetts†#	May 1, 2008	Date application received
Michigan	March 1, 2008	Date application received
Minnesota	30 days after term starts	Date application received
Mississippi	September 15, 2008	Date processed
		MTAG and MESG Grants
	March 31, 2008	HELP scholarships
Missouri	April 1, 2008	Date application received
Montana#	March 1, 2008	Date application received
New Hampshire	May 1, 2008	Date application received
New Jersey†	June 1, 2008	Tuition Aid Grant recipients (date received)
	October 1, 2008	All other applicants (date received)
	March 1, 2009	(spring term only)
New York*†	May 1, 2009	Date application received
North Carolina	March 15, 2008	Date application received
North Dakota	March 15, 2008	Date application received
Ohio	October 1, 2008	Date application received
Oklahoma#	April 15, 2008	Date application received
Pennsylvania*	May 1, 2008	Degree program recipients
	August 1, 2008	Other applicants
Rhode Island	March 1, 2008	Date application received
South Carolina	June 30, 2008	Date application received
Tennessee	May 1, 2008	Date application processed
	September 1, 2008, for state lottery	Date received
West Virginia*†	March 1, 2008	Date application received

*These states may require a supplemental form in addition to the FAFSA.
†Applicants are encouraged to obtain proof of mailing.
#For priority consideration, submit application by date specified.

For states not mentioned above, applicants are directed to contact their state higher education agency to obtain deadline information.

Institutional Aid Available Through Colleges

Although the federal government may be the largest single source of financial assistance for families, a significant amount of aid comes from the colleges themselves. Private colleges offer a variety of forms of institutional aid; public colleges generally have fewer resources to make institution-based awards to students (but remember that taxpayer support makes tuition lower at these schools). Some colleges award grants ("scholarships" or "gift aid" are other terms they may use) solely on the basis of financial need. Others award grants on the basis of need and/or "merit" as determined by that institution. For example, there may be funds available to outstanding scholars, musicians, athletes, and the like.

Many campuses also have structured student employment programs to supplement the opportunities available through the Federal Work-Study program. These college-funded job programs may be based on student skills rather than student need, although some colleges do reserve these jobs exclusively for students with financial need.

Finally, college-sponsored long-term, short-term, and emergency loans are often available to all students. The best source of information about what institutional aid might be available is the financial aid office at each college your child is considering.

 There's just not as much aid available as there used to be.

Perhaps when you went to college, you had all your higher education costs covered by outside sources. More likely, you didn't. Nonetheless, the myth persists that there simply is less money in "the system" to help pay for college these days. Actually, the reverse is true. In 1965, $558 *million* was available for financial aid. In 2006, more than $134 *billion* was available. As college costs have risen, so has the amount of money available to finance a college education. The kernel of truth in this myth is that the proportion of gift aid and self-help funding has shifted: loans and work make up a larger percentage of aid packages than they once did. That's why it's to your advantage to research as completely as possible the financing options available to your child at each of the colleges he or she is considering.

For more information about sources of financial aid:

College admissions and financial aid offices

College and university Web sites on the Internet

College Board on the Web: www.collegeboard.com

U.S. Department of Education: www.ed.gov

Guide to Getting Financial Aid 2008

The College Board Scholarship Handbook 2008. Lists more than 2,100 private and public scholarships, grants, loans, and internships covering more than 1.4 million awards. Scholarships are indexed by majors/careers, ethnicity, gender, etc. Updated annually. Available in bookstores and in libraries.

High school counselors

State scholarship/grant and loan programs

Questions Families Should Ask Colleges About Financial Aid Funding Sources

1. Will applying for financial aid have an effect on the admissions decision at this institution?

2. Does this college meet the full demonstrated need of admitted students?

3. Does the college offer institutionally funded gift aid? What percentage of freshman aid recipients receive such aid?

4. Are merit scholarships available? Are these awarded with or without regard to financial need? What percentage of freshmen receive merit scholarships?

5. Are there other special scholarships available that are awarded without regard to financial need?

6. What is the typical proportion of grant to loan in financial aid packages? Does the college give preferential aid packages (more grant, less loan) to some students? Which ones?

7. What is the typical number of hours per week that students must work to fulfill their work-study obligation?

8. Are work-study jobs readily available to financial aid recipients?

9. Are campus jobs available to students without regard to financial need?

10. Are college-sponsored long-term loans available? Is financial need a criterion?

11. What is the average loan debt accumulated during the undergraduate years by students at this college?

12. How are any outside scholarships that my child might be awarded treated in the award process? Do they reduce grant or self-help funding?

How Much Will We Be Expected to Pay?

Now that you are aware of the various financial aid sources that may be available to you to help meet college costs, you'll want to get a handle on how much you might be expected to pay. Most simply put, you and your child have the primary responsibility to pay for college expenses. There is no one right answer to the question of how much any particular family can "afford" to pay for college. However, the goal of the financial aid office is to treat families fairly in relation to others in similar circumstances, as well as in relation to those with more resources and those with less.

A need-analysis formula is used to produce an "expected family contribution" or EFC—the family's share of college costs. This family contribution is not something most families can realistically pay out of one year's income. Rather, most families finance their share of college costs through a combination of saving, paying out of current income, and borrowing.

Colleges use two standard formulas for determining how much your family will be expected to pay:

➡ **Federal Methodology (FM)**, based on the information captured on the Free Application for Federal Student Aid (FAFSA) and used by federal and state governments, and by colleges, for awarding federal and state financial aid.

➡ **Institutional Methodology (IM)**, based on the information collected on the CSS/Financial Aid PROFILE® (a Web-based financial aid form produced by the College Board) and/or college-specific financial aid applications, and used by many colleges to award institutional financial aid funds.

 Financial aid administrators at the colleges to which your child is applying use their professional judgment along with the standard formulas to determine your eligibility for financial aid. You'll want to report your financial situation as completely and accurately as possible so that your expected family contribution reflects your family's circumstances.

Determining the Expected Family Contribution (EFC)
The Parents' Contribution
Income

Both Federal Methodology and Institutional Methodology base their calculations on the parents' total income for the calendar year prior to the one in which the student will enroll. Parents' wages and all other income (such as interest, dividends, social security, and child support) are considered. The IM (but not the FM) adjusts the parents' Adjusted Gross Income (AGI), disallowing losses that are permitted in the federal tax system but that don't really affect a family's capacity to pay for college.

Not all of the family's income is considered available for college expenses because much of it must be used for basic living expenses such as housing, food, clothing, and the like. Aid administrators using the IM also take into account unusually high medical bills and, in some cases, tuition payments for children enrolled in private elementary or secondary school. If there are younger children in the family, the IM also protects a portion of the family's total income in recognition that a family must save for the educational expenses of younger children at the same time they are sending older children to college.

After subtracting taxes and other appropriate allowances from total income, a portion of the remaining "available income" is tapped for college expenses. Similar to the federal income tax structure, both the FM and IM apply a lower assessment rate to the first dollars of available income and progressively higher rates to additional dollars of available income. The more available income a family has, the more the parents will be expected to pay.

 My income is too high; we'll never qualify for aid.

While income is certainly a key factor in determining whether a family qualifies for financial aid, it is not the only one. Your assets (or lack of assets), unusually high medical or other necessary expenses, the number of family members in college at the same time, private elementary or secondary school tuition payments, and other factors are often taken into account by college financial aid administrators. Many college students receiving aid come from families whose incomes are much higher than you might expect.

Assets

You'll find that aid formulas take assets into account as well because families with assets are in a stronger financial position than families with the same income but no assets. This is true whether a family's assets are liquid or tied up in the family's home. While no one wants a family to sell their home in order to pay for college, the homeowner is in a stronger financial position than the renter. The homeowner pays lower income taxes, has stable mortgage payments, and may be able to tap into the equity in the home to finance a portion of college expenses.

It is true that a family's expected contribution is somewhat higher if there are assets than it would be if the family had not saved at all. However, a family that has saved is in a much better position than a family that must finance the expected contribution out of current income and loans. The need-analysis system considers only a very small percentage of a family's assets as available to pay for college.

It is not practical to include all categories of assets in the calculation of the family contribution, but the IM definition is as comprehensive as possible. Savings, investments, and assets held in Coverdell Savings Accounts, college savings plans, and tuition prepayment plans (including parents' assets held in the names of the students' siblings) are taken into account. The IM also considers the equity in other financial assets, including the home, other real estate, and business and farm assets. (The FM **excludes** equity in the home, in the family farm if the family lives on the farm, and in family-owned businesses with less than 100 FTE employees.)

Again, you will not be expected to use all your assets to pay for your child's education. The IM protects a portion of assets for emergencies, and also protects educational savings you have accumulated for your children's college expenses. The FM protects a portion of your assets for retirement. Both the IM and FM also protect a substantial portion of assets you may have tied up in a business or farm because they are sources of future income. After allowances are deducted, you will be expected to use only a small portion of your remaining assets for educational costs—usually about 3 to 5 percent of the total amount.

 I'll have to sell my house to pay for college.

Although many colleges will consider your home equity in determining how much you will be expected to pay, they will not expect you to sell your home. The larger portion of what your family will be expected to pay will come from your income, not your assets. At a maximum, 5 percent of the value of a portion of parents' assets (including home equity, savings, stocks and bonds, and the like) will be considered "available" to help meet college costs. You may find that you can tap into the equity in your home by borrowing against it to help finance your expected contribution, and you may receive an added benefit of deducting payments on your federal income tax return. And remember, home value is not even considered in determining eligibility for the federal student aid programs.

When More Than One Child Is Enrolled in College

As with everything else in life, families with more than one child pay more for goods and services (blue jeans, child care, ballet lessons, etc.). Similarly, families with more than one child, regardless of the spacing of those children, must make an even greater effort to plan for college financing. However, the system recognizes the particular strain on families that have two children in college at the same time and reduces the expected contribution for each child when more than one is enrolled. The IM expects the family to pay only 60 percent of the parent contribution for each child if two are enrolled. (The IM expects the parents to pay somewhat more than does the FM when more than one child is enrolled.)

Neither the FM nor the IM standard formulas consider the costs associated with the parent's enrollment in college, since many parents enrolled in college attend less than half-time or have their costs covered by employer educational benefit programs.

 Some colleges take into account the relative costs of the colleges attended by the applicant's siblings and do not divide the contribution equally among the children. Rather, they apportion the contribution. For example, if the applicant's sister is attending a low-cost community college, a higher-cost private college will expect that most of the computed contribution will be available to the student at the high-cost school.

Divorced Parents

Both Federal Methodology and Institutional Methodology take into account only the financial situation of the biological parent with whom the child has spent the greatest amount of time in the calendar year prior to college enrollment. This parent is commonly referred to as the **custodial parent**. In addition, if the custodial parent has remarried, the stepparent's financial information is also considered.

Divorced, separated, and single-parent households have become more prevalent in our society. As a result, an increasing number of students from single-parent households are seeking financial aid for college. This is understandable: families who have endured the end of a marriage or who have raised children in a single-family household frequently experience long-term financial hardships resulting from the loss of one parent's income and the division of assets.

However, regardless of the custodial arrangements, many colleges feel that it is imperative to examine the financial resources of **both** biological or adoptive parents. These schools adhere to the principle that both parents, regardless of their current marital status, have the primary responsibility for providing for their child's education and should be expected to provide reasonable financial support before college grant resources are used. This is because the financial aid system has been built on the premise of **equity**: Applicants with similar financial situations should be treated in the same way. More often than not, the noncustodial parent has some financial ability to assist with the costs of higher education. The assessment of the financial resources of the noncustodial parent is therefore a necessary part of the financial aid application process at many institutions.

Institutions are continually striving to find ways to adequately address the special needs of the divorced/separated/never-married family. Colleges recognize the need for privacy and confidentiality. However, the determination of eligibility for institutional aid requires that both parents submit documentation about their financial resources. As a result, many schools use either the College Board's online **Noncustodial PROFILE Application** or, alternatively, the paper **Noncustodial Parent's Statement** to gather the financial data needed to calculate this parent's ability to pay for the student's education.

Most schools that collect noncustodial parent financial data calculate a parental contribution using the Institutional Methodology. Recognizing the extra expenses of the noncustodial household, most institutions will make special allowances for child support paid, maintenance of two households, and the extra expenses incurred to support a new family if the noncustodial parent has remarried. In the case of remarriage, the noncustodial parent's spouse will also be asked to provide financial information.

If you are asked to provide noncustodial parent data in order to be considered for institutional grant aid, it is in your best interest to submit the required form by the institutional deadline. The student completing the PROFILE Application will be notified online if the Noncustodial PROFILE Application is required. For schools that do not use the Noncustodial PROFILE Application, the paper Noncustodial Parent's Statement will be provided directly to the student if it is required. It is the applicant's responsibility to forward application instructions to the noncustodial parent.

The information provided by the noncustodial parent will always remain **confidential** and will not be shared with the applicant or the custodial parent unless specific permission is granted. It should be noted that financial information about the custodial household also remains confidential and will not be discussed with the noncustodial parent.

Many schools will not waive the request for the noncustodial parent information even when contact with this parent has been infrequent. If you are asked to provide this data, it is best to cooperate with the institution's request so as not to forgo the opportunity to qualify for grant aid. In rare instances, the request for the form may be waived when an independent party can document that contact with the noncustodial parent is not possible. These circumstances may include cases of documented physical and emotional abuse or psychological illness. However, it is up to each institution to determine its own policies for waiving the noncustodial parent form. It is best to check with each office separately if you feel there are grounds for waiving the form.

➡ Make note of the institutional policy regarding the noncustodial parent. If this supplemental application is required (either the Noncustodial PROFILE Application or the paper Noncustodial Parent's Statement), forward it as soon as possible to your parent in order to meet institutional deadlines for funding.

➡ Speak to your financial aid office directly if you have questions about how the contribution level from the noncustodial parent will be assessed. Each institution may calculate this figure in slightly different ways.

➡ Clarify with the aid office the procedures regarding confidentiality and privacy.

➡ Don't assume that an institution will waive the requirement to submit information on the grounds that you have minimal contact with the noncustodial parent. This is generally not the case. Most colleges adhere to the principle that both parents have a responsibility to assist with education costs.

➡ If you feel you have legitimate grounds for waiving the form, contact each financial aid office at the schools to which you are applying directly. Provide written documentation about your situation and be prepared to provide information from an independent third party who is familiar with your situation.

Federal Methodology Variations

The FM provides two formula variations, depending on the level of parent taxable income and federal tax (IRS) filing status. For parents and students who file or are eligible to file IRS 1040A or 1040EZ forms, or who aren't required to file income tax forms, or are required to file but also receive means-tested federal benefits, no assets are included in the FM calculation if the parents' taxable income is less than $50,000. In instances where parents file or are eligible to file 1040A or 1040EZ forms, or aren't required to file income tax forms, or are required to file and receive means-tested federal benefits and have taxable income of $20,000 or less, the FM Expected Family Contribution is automatically reduced to zero. (The Institutional Methodology has no such variations. Its formula is applied consistently, regardless of family income and asset levels.)

We shouldn't have saved for college—our child would have qualified for more aid.

Families that have saved for college have much greater flexibility about how they pay their share of college expenses. Their lifestyle may not be significantly altered; they may have to borrow less; they will have less concern about limiting their children's college choices based on the amount of financial aid available. And for families that begin saving for college while their children are still young, a relatively modest monthly savings account for college will grow dramatically by the time the college years arrive. So be glad you saved for college—you'll probably enjoy your child's college years more than families that didn't save! (In recognition of the need for families to save for their children's college education, the Institutional Methodology will protect significant amounts of family assets from assessment for college expenses. This asset protection is based on the assumption that the parents have saved a percent of their income each year from the child's birth through senior year in high school.)

The Student's Contribution
Income and Assets

Your child's income for the previous year, as well as his or her assets (generally savings or investments held in your child's name) will be considered in a similar manner to yours. Because your child is the member of the college financing partnership who will benefit most directly, he or she will be expected to contribute a higher percentage of income and assets to meet college costs than you will. Students are expected to contribute between 22–46 percent of their available income under IM (depending on parental income) and 50 percent of their available income under FM. Dependent students are asked to contribute between 20 and 25 percent of their assets each year toward meeting college costs.

The Federal and Institutional Methodologies differ in their expectations of the student contribution from income. Under FM, students earning up to $3,080 (including income from assets) during the calendar year prior to enrollment are not expected to make any contribution from income. Under IM, the student's contribution is expected to be at least $1,550 (higher at some colleges).

Independent or Dependent?

If your child is considered independent of you for financial aid consideration, your finances will not be taken into account in determining the federal family contribution. (Some institutions, for purposes of awarding their institutional aid, may require parent information, regardless of the student's dependency status.) To be considered independent for federal financial aid purposes, your child must answer "yes" to at least one of these six questions:

➡ Is the student 24 or older?

➡ Is the student married?

➡ Is the student enrolled in a graduate or professional school program?

➡ Does the student have dependents other than a spouse?

➡ Is the student an orphan or ward of the court?

➡ Is the student a military veteran or is he or she currently serving on active duty for purposes other than training?

The FM and IM formulas treat independent students differently from students who are dependent on their parents. The case studies in this book illustrate dependent student circumstances. However, worksheets for independent student calculations are included at the end of the chapter.

Eligibility for Aid

In general, you are considered eligible for aid if there is a difference between the cost of attendance at the colleges your child is considering (see Chapter 2) and your expected family contribution. This difference is referred to as your "demonstrated financial need." The specific aid for which you will qualify varies by the source.

Federal Aid

Federal Pell Grants

Eligibility is determined by your federal expected family contribution. The size of the grant is based on a table produced annually by the U.S. Department of Education. Students with lower estimated family contributions receive larger grants. (Some Pell Grant recipients may also qualify for the Academic Competitiveness Grant and the National SMART Grant programs. See page 21 for more information.)

Federal SEOG

Eligibility is determined at the campus level. SEOG is intended to enhance educational opportunity for low-income students or help students with a high demonstrated need. Most colleges limit SEOG eligibility to those students who also qualify for a Federal Pell Grant.

Federal Work-Study (FWS)

Eligibility is based on demonstrated need. The determination to award FWS is made at the campus level.

Federal Perkins Loans

Eligibility is determined at the college level, with the government stipulation that these loans should go to students with "exceptional need" as defined by the college.

Subsidized Loans

Your child is eligible for a Federal Stafford Loan or a Federal Direct Loan if you have demonstrated need based on the Federal Methodology.

Unsubsidized Loans

Your child may be eligible for an unsubsidized Federal Stafford or Direct Loan regardless of whether your family demonstrates need; if you make the determination that aid from other sources is not enough to cover the cost of attendance, you may apply for these loans.

PLUS Loans

As a parent you are eligible to borrow any sum of money through the PLUS program up to the cost of attendance minus any other aid received. Your family does not have to demonstrate financial need to qualify.

State Aid

State Scholarships and Grants

Eligibility is determined by each state program, and there is some variation from one state to another. In most states, need-based scholarships and grants are awarded on the basis of the number of eligible applicants, the amount of money supporting the program, and a ranking of applicant need determined by the state's use of FM or a variation of that formula. A student's academic record and/or scores on standardized admissions tests, such as the SAT® or ACT, may also be considered in the awarding of some competitive state scholarships. State scholarships and grants are limited to qualified state residents.

State Loans

Some states have student or parent loan programs in addition to the federal loan programs described above. Check with your state financial aid agency or college financial aid offices to learn about any state-funded loan programs that might be available to you.

Institutional Aid

As you may have noticed, college financial aid administrators have some flexibility even in the awarding of federal aid to students. They have much greater latitude in awarding their own institution-sponsored aid.

You already know that many colleges use the Institutional Methodology and require that the PROFILE or other additional financial aid applications be completed, in addition to the FAFSA, so that they can gain a clearer picture of your family's financial situation. But you should also be aware that several colleges can look at the same family's information and IM results and come up with different expected family contributions and thus different figures for demonstrated financial need. As we follow up with our case studies, you will see examples of differing determinations by colleges.

What's important to keep in mind here is that institutions, not formulas, determine how institutional funds will be awarded. To plan well, it will be important for you to find out as much as you can about each college's policies for assessing the family contribution and determining eligibility for financial aid. (See Chapter 6 for more information about adjustments to IM.)

 My child isn't an A student; we'll never get aid.

While there are a significant number of merit scholarships that recognize academic talent and reward students regardless of their financial circumstances, by far the majority of financial aid awarded these days goes to students with demonstrated financial need. If your child is admitted to a college that awards most financial aid on the basis of demonstrated need, straight A's will not be the key factor in determining the amount of the award.

Expected Family Contribution and Demonstrated Need

You can use the worksheets at the end of this chapter to estimate your family's expected contribution. The following calculations of expected contributions are for the students and families you met in Chapter 2.

Sarah Smith

Two of the colleges in which Sarah is interested use only the Federal Methodology to determine eligibility for financial aid. The third college uses Federal Methodology but calculates an expected contribution from Sarah's noncustodial parent. Sarah's mother earned $44,250 in wages in 2007 and an additional $300 in taxable income (interest and dividends). She also received $10,800 in child support, which was untaxed. **The total family income was $55,350.**

From this total income figure, FM allows deductions for U.S. incomes tax, state and other taxes, and social security taxes (totaling $8,504 in Sarah's mother's case). In addition, allowances are made for employment expenses and basic living expenses (another $26,960). Altogether, $35,464 in allowances is deducted from the total family income to arrive at **$19,886 in available income**.

As for assets, Sarah's mother has $7,500 in savings and $4,000 in investment equity. Because these assets are lower than the asset protection allowance and because the family qualifies for the "simple needs test," no contribution is expected from assets. (see FM variations on page 39.) **The adjusted available income remains at $19,886.** From this, **$4,664 would be the expected parent contribution**.

As for Sarah's contribution, FM takes into account the $2,900 she earned in wages and interest income in 2007. After taking allowances for state and other taxes and income protection, Sarah's available income is $0; she will not be expected to make any contribution from income. While she does have

$1,000 in a savings account, the fact that her family qualifies for the "simple needs test" means Sarah would not be expected to make a contribution from assets.

Thus, **the total expected family contribution, under Federal Methodology, would be $4,664.00**

Parents' expected contribution: Sarah Smith	Federal Methodology
A. 2007 income	
1. Father's yearly wages, salary, tips, and other compensation	$ 0
2. Mother's yearly wages, salary, tips, and other compensation	$ 44,250
3. All other income of mother and father (dividends, social security, pensions, welfare, child support, etc.)	$ 11,100
4. IRS allowable adjustments to income (business expenses, interest penalties, alimony paid, etc.)	$ 0
B. Total income	$ 55,350
C. Total allowances against income	$ 35,464
D. Available income	$ 19,886
E. Assets	
1. Cash, savings, and checking accounts	$ 7,500
2. Other investments (current net value)	$ 4,000
F. Total assets	$ 11,500
G. Asset protection allowance	$ 17,600
H. Remaining assets	$ 0
I. Income supplement from assets	$ 0
J. Adjusted available income	$ 19,886
K. Parents' expected contribution	**$ 4,664**

James Washington

One of James's college choices uses FM to award both institutional and federal aid. His other two choices both use IM, but one school employs an alternative calculation, adjusting for higher cost of living levels in James's hometown of Boston. As you will see from the case, the IM contribution levels shown on page 47 are slightly different.

James's father earned $79,350 in salary in 2007; his parents also earned $700 in interest on investments. They received $3,000 in untaxed benefits. Thus **the total family income was $83,050**. From this total figure, both Federal

Methodology and Institutional Methodology allow deductions for U.S. income tax, state and other taxes, social security taxes, and basic living expenses. In addition to these allowances, IM considers the heavy medical expenses James's family incurred during the past year. IM also protects 1.52 percent of the Washingtons' income **($1,262)** so they can save for James's sister's college expenses. This consideration is partially responsible for the difference in the FM allowances **(totaling $40,293)** and the IM allowances **($52,378)**. Again, these differences are reflected in the two **available income** figures in the following table: **$42,757 for FM, $30,672 for IM**. In the case of the college that considers the higher cost of living in Boston, the IM allowances **total $53,728** and the **available income is $29,322.**

As for assets, James's parents have $4,500 in savings and $6,600 in investment equity. They also have invested $5,000 for each of their children in their state's college savings plan. In addition, they have $85,000 in home equity, which is taken into consideration by Institutional Methodology but not by Federal Methodology. For **FM** purposes, James's family has **$21,100 in total assets**; for **IM** purposes, the **asset total is $106,100**. FM allows for asset protection that is greater than the total assets; thus, no contribution would be expected from these assets. IM calculates an asset contribution of $1,696. James's parents would be expected to contribute **$14,549 under FM and only $9,545 under IM**. The institution using the additional COLA allowance for James's family has calculated an IM parental contribution of $9,035.

As for James's contribution, both methodologies take into account the $3,150 he earned in wages in 2007 and his $48 income from investments. After taking allowances for state and other taxes and income protection, James's available income is $0 (FM), with his expected contribution from income figured at $0 (FM). Under Institutional Methodology, no income protection is provided: after taking allowances, IM considers James's available income to be $2,588. Since IM expects a minimum student income, James' contribution is $1,550. James also has $2,000 in savings. From this, $400 would be expected under FM and $500 under IM. Thus, James's **total expected student contribution would be $400 (FM) and $2,050 (IM)**.

Adding the totals for parent and student contributions, James's **expected family contribution under FM would be $14,949; and under IM, $11,595.** Using IM with the additional cost of living allowance for Boston, **the total family contribution would be $11,085.**

Parents' expected contribution: James Washington	FM	IM
A. 2006 income		
1. Father's yearly wages, salary, tips, and other compensation	$79,350	$ 79,350
2. Mother's yearly wages, salary, tips, and other compensation	$ 0	$ 0
3. All other income of mother and father (dividends, social security, pensions, welfare, child support, etc.)	$ 3,700	$ 3,700
4. IRS allowable adjustments to income (business expenses, interest penalties, alimony paid, etc.)	$ 0	$ 0
B. Total income	$83,050	$ 83,050
C. Total allowances against income	$40,293	$ 52,378
D. Available income	$42,757	$ 30,672
E. Assets		
1. Cash, savings, and checking accounts	$ 4,500	$ 4,500
2. Other investments (current net value)	$16,600	$ 16,600
3. Home equity		$ 85,000
F. Total assets	$21,100	$106,100
G. Asset protection allowances	$46,400	$ 55,984
H. Remaining assets	$ 0	$ 50,116
I. Parents' expected contribution	**$14,549**	**$ 9,545**

Maria Martinez

Both of the private colleges in which Maria is interested use IM to determine eligibility for institutional funds. The public college uses FM. Maria's father earned $93,900 in salary in 2007; her mother earned $96,500. In addition, her parents earned $3,150 in interest on investments. They also had $4,000 in untaxed income, which represented their retirement contribution. Thus, the **total family income was $197,550**.

From this total figure, both Federal Methodology and Institutional Methodology allow deductions for U.S. income tax, state and other taxes, social security taxes, and basic living expenses. In addition to these allowances, IM protects a portion of the Martinez family's income ($9,880) so they can save for each of the four younger children's college expenses. This consideration results in the difference between the FM allowances (totaling $89,943) and IM allowances (totaling $109,620). This difference is reflected in the two **available income** figures in the following table: **$107,607 for FM** and **$87,930 for IM**.

As for assets, Maria's parents have $22,000 in savings and $53,000 in investment equity. They also have $176,000 in home equity, which is taken into
consideration by Institutional Methodology but not by Federal Methodology.
For **FM** purposes, Maria's family has **$75,000 in total assets**; for **IM** pur-
poses, the **asset total is $251,000**. From these assets, both methodolo-
gies allow for protection that is *less* than the total assets. The IM allowance
$222,525 includes considerable protection for savings for the six children's
college educations, as well as protection for emergencies. The FM allowance
protects $51,800 of the Martinez family's assets for retirement and education
costs. Taking into account that Maria's brother is attending college full-time,
**$23,168 would be expected as the FM contribution; $20,482 as the
expected parent contribution under IM**.

As for Maria's contribution, both methodologies take into account the $1,850
she earned in wages in 2007 and her $100 income from investments. After
taking allowances for state and other taxes and income protection, Maria's
available income is $0 (FM). Under Institutional Methodology, no income pro-
tection is provided: after taking allowances, IM considers Maria's available
income to be $0. Since IM sets a minimum of $1,550 as the student contribution, $1,550 would be expected as Maria's contribution from income, based
on a combination of 2007 and assumed 2008 earnings. Maria also has $2,500
in savings. From this, $500 would be expected under FM and $625 under IM.
Thus, Maria's **total expected student contribution would be $500 (FM)
and $2,175 under IM**.

Adding the totals for parent and student contributions, Maria's **expected
family contribution under FM would be $23,668; and $22,657 under
IM**.

Parents' expected contribution: Maria Martinez	FM	IM
A. 2007 income		
1. Father's yearly wages, salary, tips, and other compensation	$ 93,900	$ 93,900
2. Mother's yearly wages, salary, tips, and other compensation	$ 96,500	$ 96,500
3. All other income of mother and father (dividends, social security, pensions, welfare, child support, etc.)	$ 7,150	$ 7,150
4. IRS allowable adjustments to income (business expenses, interest penalties, alimony paid, etc.)	$ 0	$ 0
B. Total income	$197,550	$197,550
C. Total allowances against income	$ 89,943	$109,620
D. Available income	$107,607	$ 87,930
E. Assets		
1. Cash, savings, and checking accounts	$ 22,000	$ 22,000
2. Other investments (current net value)	$ 53,000	$ 53,000
3. Home equity		$176,000
F. Total assets	$ 75,000	$251,000
G. Asset protection allowance	$ 51,800	$185,428
H. Remaining assets	$ 23,200	$ 65,572
I. **Parents' contribution if two family members in college**	**$ 23,168**	**$ 20,482**

For more information on calculating family contributions:

College and university Web sites

College Board on the Web: www.collegeboard.com

Guide to Getting Financial Aid 2008

College financial aid offices

Questions Families Should Ask About How Their
Expected Contribution Will Be Determined

The following questions relate to how each of the colleges your child is
considering will determine your expected contribution toward that college's
costs, and thus your demonstrated need, if any, for college-sponsored funds.
You'll be able to get answers to these questions from financial aid administrators at your child's college choices.

1. What methodology or formula does this college use in deter-
    mining financial need for college-sponsored aid programs?

2. If the college uses an Institutional Methodology, what
    college-specific adjustments are made, if any?

3. Does the college consider the noncustodial parent's income
    and assets? If so, does the college also consider the
    stepparent's income and assets?

4. What is the minimum student contribution expected by the
    college?

5. Does the college consider medical or dental expenses?

6. Does the college make an allowance for elementary or
    secondary school tuition costs for younger children in the
    family?

7. What is the college's policy about treatment of business or
    farm assets?

8. Does the college consider home assets? If so, how?

9. Does the college consider costs of the parents' college
    enrollment?

10. How does the college adjust the contribution to account for
    the costs of a sibling's college enrollment?

2008–2009 Federal Methodology (FM) Worksheet
Parent(s) of Dependent Student

Student's Name:	**Social Security Number:**	

Parents' Income		
1. AGI/taxable income		$
2. Untaxed income and benefits	+	
3. Income exclusions (child support paid + education tax credits)	-	
4. Total parents' income (sum of lines 1 and 2, minus line 3)	=	
Allowances		
5. U.S. income tax		
6. State and other taxes (% from Table 1 x line 4)	+	
7. F.I.C.A. (Table 2)	+	
8. Employment allowance (Table 2)	+	
9. Income protection allowance (Table 3a)	+	
10. Total allowances (sum of lines 5–9)	=	
11. Available income (line 4 minus line 10)	=	
Parents' Assets*		
12. Cash, savings, and checking accounts		
13. Other real estate/investment equity	+	
14. Adjusted business/farm equity (Table 4)**	+	
15. Net worth (sum of lines 12–14)	=	
16. Education Savings and Asset protection allowance (Table 5)	-	
17. Discretionary net worth (line 15 minus line 16)	=	
18. Conversion percentage	x	12%
19. Contribution from assets (line 17 x line 18; if simple-needs test or line 17 is negative, enter $0)	=	
20. Adjusted available income (sum of line 11 and line 19)	=	
Contribution***		
21. Total contribution (calculate using line 20 and Table 8)	=	
22. Number of dependent children in college at least half-time	÷	
23. Parents' contribution for student (line 21 divided by line 22; if negative, enter $0)	=	

* For parents who are not required to file or who are eligible to file an IRS 1040A or 1040EZ, or who are required to file a 1040 form but also receive means-tested federal benefits, no assets are included in the methodology if parents' AGI is less than $50,000.

** Business equity is excluded if business has fewer than 100 employees or FTE employees; family farms are excluded.

***For parents who are not required to file or who are eligible to file an IRS 1040A or 1040EZ, or who are required to file a 1040 form but also receive means-tested federal benefits and whose AGI is less than $20,000, no contribution is expected.

2008–2009 Federal Methodology (FM) Worksheet
Dependent Student

Student's Name:		Social Security Number:		

Student's Income				
1. AGI/taxable income				$
2. Untaxed income and benefits			+	
3. Taxable student aid			-	
4. Total income (sum of lines 1 and 2, minus line 3)			=	
Allowances				
5. U.S. income tax				
6. State and other taxes (% from Table 1 x line 4)			+	
7. F.I.C.A. (Table 2)			+	
8. Income protection allowance (Table 3c)			+	
9. Parents' negative available income offset (line 11 of parents' worksheet, if negative)			+	3,080
10. Total allowances (sum of lines 5–9)			=	
11. Available income (line 4 minus line 10)			=	
12. Available income assessment rate			x	0.50
13. Contribution from income (line 11 x line 12; if negative, enter $0)			=	
Student's Assets*				
14. Cash, savings, and checking accounts				
15. Other real estate/investment equity			+	
16. Business/farm equity**			+	
17. Net assets (sum of lines 14–16)			=	
18. Asset assessment rate			x	0.20
19. Contribution from assets (line 17 x line 18; if simple needs test, enter $0)			=	
Contribution***				
20. Total student contribution (sum of lines 13 and 19)			=	

* For parents who are not required to file or who are eligible to file an IRS 1040A or 1040EZ, or who are required to file a 1040 form but also receive means-tested federal benefits, no assets are included in the methodology if parents' AGI is less than $50,000.

** Business equity is excluded if business has fewer than 100 employees or FTE employees; family farms are excluded.

*** For parents who are not required to file or who are eligible to file an IRS 1040A or 1040EZ, or who are required to file a 1040 form but also receive means-tested federal benefits and whose AGI is less than $20,000, no contribution is expected.

2008–2009 Federal Methodology (FM) Worksheet
Independent Student with Dependents

Student's Name:		Social Security Number:		

Student's (and Spouse's) Income				
1.	AGI/taxable income			$
2.	Untaxed income and benefits		+	
3.	Income exclusions (child support paid + taxable student aid + education tax credits)		-	
4.	**Total income (sum of lines 1 and 2, minus line 3)**		=	
Allowances				
5.	U.S. income tax			
6.	State and other taxes (% from Table 1 x line 4)		+	
7.	F.I.C.A. (Table 2)		+	
8.	Employment allowance (Table 2)		+	
9.	Income protection allowance (Table 3b)		+	
10.	Total allowances (sum of lines 5–9)		=	
11.	**Available income (line 4 minus line 10)**		=	
Student's (and Spouse's) Assets*				
12.	Cash, savings, and checking accounts			
13.	Other real estate/investment equity		+	
14.	Adjusted business/farm equity (Table 4)**		+	
15.	**Net worth (sum of lines 12–14)**		=	
16.	Education savings and asset protection allowance (Table 5)		-	
17.	**Discretionary net worth (line 15 minus line 16)**		=	
18.	Conversion percentage		X	7%
19.	Contribution from assets (line 17 x line 18; if simple needs test or line 17 is negative, enter 0)		=	
20.	**Adjusted available income (sum of lines 11 and line 19)**		=	
Contribution*				
21.	**Total contribution (calculate using line 20 and Table 8)**		=	
22.	Number of family members enrolled at least half-time		÷	
23.	**Student contribution (line 21 divided by line 22; if negative, enter 0)**		=	

* For students (and their spouse, if married) who are not required to file or who are eligible to file an IRS 1040A or 1040EZ, or who file or are required to file a 1040 form but also receive means-tested federal benefits, no assets are included in the methodology if the AGI is less than $50,000.

** Business equity is excluded if business has fewer than 100 employees or FTE employees; family farms are excluded.

***For students (and their spouse, if married) who are not required to file or who are eligible to file an IRS 1040A or 1040EZ, or who file or are required to file a 1040 form but also receive means-tested federal benefits and whose AGI is less than or equal to $20,000, no contribution is expected.

2008–2009 Federal Methodology (FM) Worksheet
Independent Student Without Dependents

Student's Name:	Social Security Number:		

Student's Income			
1. AGI/taxable income			$
2. Untaxed income and benefits		+	
3. Income exclusions (child support paid + taxable student aid + education tax credits)		-	
4. Total income (sum of lines 1 and 2, minus line 3)		=	
Allowances			
5. U.S. income tax			
6. State and other taxes (% from Table 1 x line 4)		+	
7. F.I.C.A. (Table 2)		+	
8. Employment allowance (Table 2)		+	
9. Income protection allowance (Table 3c)		+	
10. Total allowances (sum of lines 5–9)		=	
11. Available income (line 4 minus line 10)		=	
12. Available income assessment rate			0.50
13. Student's contribution from income (line 11 x line 12)		=	
Student's (and Spouse's) Assets			
14. Cash, savings, and checking accounts			
15. Other real estate/investment equity		+	
16. Adjusted business/farm equity (Table 4)		+	
17. Net worth (sum of lines 14–16)		=	
18. Asset protection allowance (Table 5)		-	
19. Discretionary net worth (line 17 minus line 18)		=	
20. Asset assessment rate		x	0.20
21. Contribution from assets (line 19 x line 20; if simple needs test or line 19 is negative, enter 0)		=	
Contribution			
22. Total contribution (line 13 and line 21)		=	
23. Number in college		÷	
24. Student contribution (line 22 divided by line 23; if negative, enter 0)		=	

2008–2009
Federal Methodology (FM)
Computation Tables

TABLE 1. ALLOWANCES FOR STATE AND OTHER TAXES			TABLE 1., *continued*		
	Parents of Dependent Students and Independent Students with Dependents Other than a Spouse	Dependent Students and Independent w/ No Dependents		Parents of Dependent Students and Independent Students with Dependents Other than a Spouse	Dependent Students and Independent w/ No Dependents
	Total Income	**Total Income**		**Total Income**	**Total Income**
State/Territory/Country of Residence	$ 0– 14,999	15,000– or more	Any amount	*State/Territory/Country of Residence*	$ 0– 14,999	15,000– or more	Any amount

State/Territory/Country	$ 0–14,999	15,000– or more	Any amount	State/Territory/Country	$ 0–14,999	15,000– or more	Any amount
Alabama (AL)	3%	2%	2%	Texas (TX)	3%	2%	1%
Alaska (AK)	2	1	0	Utah (UT)	5	4	4
American Samoa (AS)	3	2	2	Vermont (VT)	5	4	3
Arizona (AZ)	4	3	3	Virgin Islands (VI)	3	2	2
Arkansas (AR)	4	3	3	Virginia (VA)	5	4	3
California (CA)	7	6	5	Washington (WA)	4	3	2
Canada (CN)	3	2	2	West Virginia (WV)	3	2	2
Colorado (CO)	4	3	3	Wisconsin (WI)	7	6	4
Connecticut (CT)	7	6	4	Wyoming (WY)	2	1	1
Delaware (DE)	4	3	3	Not Reported (NR)	3	2	2
District of Columbia (DC)	7	6	6				

TABLE 2. ALLOWANCES AGAINST INCOME

Federated States of Micronesia (FM)	3	2	2
Florida (FL)	3	2	1
Georgia (GA)	6	5	3
Guam (GU)	3	2	2
Hawaii (HI)	4	3	4
Idaho (ID)	5	4	3
Illinois (IL)	5	4	2
Indiana (IN)	4	3	3
Iowa (IA)	5	4	3
Kansas (KS)	5	4	3
Kentucky (KY)	5	4	4
Louisiana (LA)	3	2	2
Maine (ME)	6	5	4
Marshall Islands (MH)	3	2	2
Maryland (MD)	7	6	5
Massachusetts (MA)	6	5	4
Mexico (MX)	3	2	2
Michigan (MI)	5	4	3
Minnesota (MN)	6	5	4
Mississippi	4	3	2
Missouri (MO)	5	4	3
Montana (MT)	5	4	3
Nebraska (NE)	5	4	3
Nevada (NV)	3	2	1
New Hampshire (NH)	5	4	1
New Jersey (NJ)	8	7	4
New Mexico (NM)	4	3	3
New York (NY)	9	8	6
North Carolina (NC)	6	5	4
North Dakota (ND)	2	1	1
Northern Mariana Islands (MP)	3	2	2
Ohio (OH)	6	5	4
Oklahoma (OK)	6	5	3
Oregon (OR)	7	6	5
Palau (PW)	3	2	2
Pennsylvania (PA)	5	4	3
Puerto Rico (PR)	3	2	2
Rhode Island (RI)	7	6	4
South Carolina (SC)	5	4	3
South Dakota (SD)	2	1	1
Tennessee (TN)	2	1	1

FICA: Wages

$1 to $97,500	7.65% of income earned by each wage earner (maximum of $7,312.50 per person)
$97,501 or more	$7,312.50 + 1.45% of income earned above $97,500 by each wage earner
Employment allowance	35% of lesser earned income to a maximum of $3,300 (single parent: 35% of earned income to a maximum of $3,300)

TABLE 3a. INCOME PROTECTION ALLOWANCE (IPA)
(Parents of Dependent Students)

Family Size* (including student)	Number in College**				
	1	2	3	4	5
2	$15,380	12,750			
3	19,150	16,540	13,900		
4	23,660	21,020	18,410	15,770	
5	27,910	25,280	22,660	20,030	17,410
6	32,650	30,010	27,400	24,770	22,150

*For each additional family member, add $3,680.
**For each additional college student, subtract $2,620.

TABLE 3b. INCOME PROTECTION ALLOWANCE (IPA)
(Independent Students with Dependents Other Than A Spouse)

Family Size* (including student)	Number in College**				
	1	2	3	4	5
2	$15,750	13,060			
3	19,610	16,930	14,240		
4	24,220	21,530	18,850	16,150	
5	28,580	25,880	23,200	20,510	17,830
6	33,420	30,730	28,060	25,350	22,680

*For each additional family member, add $3,770.
**For each additional college student, subtract $2,680.

2008–2009
Federal Methodology (FM)
Computation Tables

TABLE 3c. INCOME PROTECTION ALLOWANCE
(Dependent Students and Independent Students
without Dependents)

Dependent Student $3,080	
Independent Student 6,220	
Married Independent	
(student and spouse enrolled) 6,220	
Married Independent	
(only student is enrolled) 9,970	

TABLE 4. ADJUSTED NET WORTH OF A BUSINESS OR FARM

Net Worth (NW)	Adjusted Net Worth
Less than $1	$ 0
$ 1 to 110,000	$ 0 + 40% of NW
$ 110,001 to 330,000	$ 44,000 + 50% of NW over $110,000
$ 330,001 to 550,000	$ 154,000 + 60% of NW over $330,000
$ 550,001 or more	$ 286,000 + 100% of NW over $550,000

TABLE 5. EDUCATION SAVINGS AND ASSET PROTECTION ALLOWANCE
(Parents of Independent Students)

Age of older parent of student	Couple/ Married	Unmarried/ Single
25 or under ....$ 0		$ 0
26	2,600	1,100
27	5,100	2,100
28	7,700	3,200
29	10,200	4,300
30	12,800	5,300
31	15,400	6,400
32	17,900	7,500
33	20,500	8,500
34	23,000	9,600
35	25,600	10,700
36	28,200	11,700
37	30,700	12,800
38	33,300	13,900
39	35,800	14,900
40	38,400	16,000
41	39,300	16,400
42	40,300	16,700
43	41,300	17,100
44	42,300	17,600
45	43,400	17,900
46	44,500	18,300
47	45,600	18,800
48	46,700	19,200
49	47,900	19,700
50	49,000	20,100
51	50,500	20,500
52	51,800	21,000
53	53,300	21,500
54	54,600	22,100
55	56,300	22,600
56	57,600	23,200
57	59,300	23,700
58	61,100	24,400
59	62,900	25,000
60	64,700	25,700
61	66,600	26,300
62	68,500	27,000
63	70,800	27,800
64	72,800	28,500
65 or over	75,200	29,300

TABLE 6. ASSET CONVERSION ALLOWANCE
(Parents of Dependent Students/Independent Students
without Dependents Other than a Spouse)

Asset conversion rate for Dependent Students and Independent Students without Dependents is 20%.

Asset conversion rate for Parents is 12%.

Asset conversion rate for Independent Students with Dependents is 7%.

TABLE 7. INCOME ASSESSMENT RATE
(Dependent Students/Independent Students
without Dependents)

50% of available income

TABLE 8. CONTRIBUTION FROM ADJUSTED AVAILABLE INCOME (AAI)
(Parents of Dependent Students/Independent Students
without Dependents Other than a Spouse)

Adjusted Available Income (AAI)	Total Contributions from Income
Less than $ -3,409	$ -750
$ -3,409 to 13,700	22% of AAI
$ 13,701 to 17,300 ....$ 3,014 + 25% of AAI over $ 13,700
$ 17,301 to 20,800 ....$ 3,914 + 29% of AAI over $ 17,300
$ 20,801 to 24,300 ....$ 4,929 + 34% of AAI over $ 20,800
$ 24,301 to 27,800 ....$ 6,119 + 40% of AAI over $ 24,300
$ 27,801 or more ....$ 7,519 + 47% of AAI over $ 27,800

2008–2009 Institutional Methodology (IM) Worksheet
Parent(s) of Dependent Students

Student's Name:		Social Security Number:		
Income of Parent(s)				
1. AGI/taxable income				$
a. Add back losses from business, farm, etc., and capital losses			+	
2. Untaxed income and benefits			+	
3. Child support paid			-	
4. Total parents' income (sum of lines 1, 1a, and 2, minus 3)			=	
Allowances				
5. U.S. income tax				
6. State and other taxes (% from Table 1 x line 4)			+	
7. F.I.C.A. (Table 2)			+	
8. Medical/dental expense allowance (Table 2)			+	
9. Employment allowance (Table 2)			+	
10. Annual education savings allowance (AESA) (Table 4):				
a. Annual savings goal (1.52% x line 4, up to $2,470)	=			
b. Number of precollege children, excluding student	x			
c. Total AESA (line 10a x 10b)			+	
11. Income protection allowance (Table 3a)			+	
12. Total allowances (sum of lines 5–11)			=	
13. Available income (line 4 minus line 12)			=	
14. Total PC from income (calculate using line 13 and Table 5; if negative, enter $0)			=	
Assets				
15. Cash, savings, and checking accounts				
16. Home equity			+	
17. Investment equity			+	
18. Other real estate equity			+	
19. Adjusted business/farm equity (Table 7)			+	
20. Parental assets in siblings' names				
21. Net worth (sum of lines 15–20)			=	
22. Asset protection allowances:				
a. Emergency reserve allowance (Table 8):	=			
b. Cumulative education savings allowance (CESA) (Table 4)	+			
c. Low income asset allowance (amount from line 13, if negative)	+			
d. Total asset protection allowances (sum of a + b + c)			-	
23. Discretionary net worth (line 21 minus line 22d, if negative, enter $0)			=	
24. Total PC from assets (calculate using line 23 and Table 9)			=	
Contribution				
25. Total parent contribution (sum of line 14 and line 24)			=	
26. Number in college adjustment (Table 10)			x	%
27. Parent contribution for student (line 25 x line 26)			=	

* The marginal rates are the percentages use in the income bands in Table 5. For example, for an available income of $35,000, the income band "$32,641 to $38,210" would be used. For this income band, the marginal rate is 38%.

2008–2009 Institutional Methodology (IM) Worksheet Dependent Student

Student's Name:	Social Security Number:		
Income of Student			
1. AGI/taxable income		$	
2. Untaxed income and benefits	+		
3. Taxable student aid	-		
4. Total income (sum of lines 1 and 2, minus 3)	=		
Allowances			
5. U.S. income tax			
6. State and other taxes (% from Table 1 x line 1)	+		
7. F.I.C.A. (Table 2)	+		
8. Total allowances (sum of lines 5–7)	=		
9. Available income (line 4 minus line 8)	=		
10. Available income assessment rate (Parents' marginal rate from Parent Worksheet, line 14.1)	x		%
11. Multiply student's available income by assessment rate (line 9 x line 10)			
12. Student standard contribution from income (Table 11)			
13. Enter higher of line 11 or line 12			
14. Total parent contribution (Parent Worksheet, line 25)			
15. Multiply by 50%	x		50%
16. Student contribution cap (line 14 x line 15)			
11. Student contribution from income (lesser of line 13 or line 16)	=		
Assets			
18. Cash, savings, and checking accounts			
19. Home equity	+		
20. Investment equity	+		
21. Other real estate equity	+		
22. Business/farm equity	+		
23. Trust value	+		
24. Net worth (sum of lines 18–23)	=		
25. Asset assessment rate	x		0.25
26. Student contribution from assets (line 24 x line 25)	=		
Contribution			
27. Total student contribution (sum of line 17 and line 26)	=		

2008–2009 Institutional Methodology (IM) Worksheet
Independent Student

Student's Name:		Social Security Number:		

Income of Student (and Spouse)			
1. AGI/taxable income			$
2. Untaxed income and benefits		+	
3. Income adjustments (child support paid + taxable student aid)		-	
4. Total family income (sum of lines 1 and 2, minus 3)		=	
Allowances			
5. U.S. income tax			
6. State and other taxes (% from Table 1 x line 1)		+	
7. F.I.C.A. (Table 2)		+	
8. Medical/dental expense allowance (Table 2)		+	
9. Employment allowance (Table 2)		+	
10. Annual education savings allowance (AESA) (Table 4):			
a. Annual savings goal (1.52% x line 4, up to $2,470)	=		
b. Number of precollege children	x		
c. Total AESA (line 10a x 10b)		+	
11. Monthly maintenance allowance (Table 3b)		+	
12. Total allowances (sum of lines 5–11)		=	
13. Available income (line 4 minus line 12)		=	
14. Available income assessment rate		x	0.70
15. SC from income (line 13 x line 14)		=	
16. Number in college adjustment (Table 10)		x	
17. SC from income for the student (line 15 x line 16)		=	
Assets			
18. Cash, savings, and checking accounts			
19. Home equity		+	
20. Investment equity		+	
21. Other real estate equity		+	
22. Adjusted business/farm equity (Table 7)		+	
23. Trust value		+	
24. Net worth (sum of lines 18–23)		=	
25. Asset protection allowances:			
a. Emergency reserve allowance (Table 8):	=		
b. Cumulative education savings allowance (CESA) (Table 4, dependent children only)	+		
c. Total asset protection allowances (sum of a + b)		=	
26. Discretionary net worth (line 24 minus line 25c—if negative, enter 0)		=	
27. Asset assessment rate		x	0.25
28. Total student contribution from assets (line 26 x line 27)		=	
29. Number in college adjustment (Table 10)		x	
30. Student contribution from assets (line 28 x line 29)		=	
Contribution			
31. Total contribution (sum of line 17 and line 30)		=	

2008-2009
Institutional Methodology (IM)
Computation Tables

TABLE 1.   ALLOWANCES FOR STATE AND OTHER TAXES

State	Parents of Dependents												Students	
	0 - 30,000	30,001 - 40,000	40,001 - 50,000	50,001 - 60,000	60,001 - 70,000	70,001 - 80,000	80,001 - 90,000	90,001 - 100,000	100,001 - 110,000	110,001 - 120,000	120,001 - 130,000	More than 130,000	0 - 20,000	More than 20,000
Alabama (AL)	9.0	9.5	9.0	8.5	8.0	7.5	7.5	7.0	6.5	6.5	6.5	6.0	2.5	3.0
Alaska (AK)	4.0	3.5	3.5	3.5	3.5	4.0	4.0	4.0	4.0	4.0	4.0	4.0	0.0	0.0
American Samoa (AS)	4.5	4.0	3.5	3.0	2.5	2.0	2.0	2.0	2.0	2.0	2.0	2.0	0.0	0.0
Arizona (AZ)	9.5	9.5	9.0	8.5	8.0	8.0	8.0	8.0	8.0	8.0	8.0	8.0	1.5	1.5
Arkansas (AR)	9.5	9.5	9.0	9.0	9.0	9.0	9.0	9.0	9.0	9.0	9.0	8.5	1.5	2.0
California (CA)	8.5	8.0	8.0	8.0	8.0	8.5	9.0	9.5	9.5	9.5	9.5	10.0	1.0	1.5
Canada (CN)	11.0	12.0	12.0	12.0	12.0	12.5	13.0	13.0	13.0	13.0	13.0	12.5	1.0	1.5
Colorado (CO)	8.0	8.0	8.0	8.0	8.0	8.5	8.5	8.5	8.5	8.5	8.5	8.0	1.5	2.0
Connecticut (CT)	11.0	12.0	12.0	12.0	12.0	12.5	13.0	13.0	13.0	13.0	13.0	12.5	1.0	1.5
Delaware (DE)	4.5	5.0	5.5	6.0	6.0	6.0	6.5	6.5	6.5	6.0	6.0	6.0	1.5	2.0
District of Columbia (DC)	8.0	8.5	9.0	9.5	9.5	9.5	9.5	9.5	10.0	10.0	10.0	9.5	2.0	2.5
Federated States of Micronesia (FM)	4.5	4.0	3.5	3.0	2.5	2.0	2.0	2.0	2.0	2.0	2.0	2.0	0.0	0.0
Florida (FL)	9.0	8.5	8.0	7.5	7.0	6.5	6.5	6.5	6.0	6.0	6.0	5.5	0.0	0.0
Guam (GU)	4.5	4.0	3.5	3.0	2.5	2.0	2.0	2.0	2.0	2.0	2.0	2.0	0.0	0.0
Georgia (GA)	9.0	9.0	9.5	9.5	9.5	9.5	9.5	9.5	9.5	9.5	9.5	9.0	2.0	2.5
Hawaii (HI)	8.0	8.0	8.0	8.0	8.0	8.0	8.0	8.0	8.0	8.0	8.0	7.5	3.0	3.5
Idaho (ID)	9.0	9.0	9.0	9.0	9.0	9.0	9.0	9.0	9.0	9.0	9.0	8.5	1.5	2.0
Illinois (IL)	11.5	11.0	10.5	10.5	10.5	10.5	10.0	10.0	10.0	10.0	10.0	9.5	1.5	2.0
Indiana (IN)	11.0	10.5	10.0	10.0	9.5	9.0	9.0	9.0	8.5	8.5	8.5	8.0	3.0	3.5
Iowa (IA)	10.5	10.5	10.5	10.5	10.0	10.0	10.0	10.0	10.0	10.0	10.0	9.5	2.0	2.5
Kansas (KS)	9.0	9.5	10.0	10.5	10.5	10.5	10.5	10.0	10.0	10.0	10.0	9.5	1.5	2.0
Kentucky (KY)	9.5	9.5	10.0	10.0	10.0	10.0	10.0	10.0	10.0	10.0	10.0	9.5	2.5	3.0
Louisiana (LA)	8.0	7.5	7.5	7.5	7.0	7.0	7.0	7.0	7.0	7.0	7.0	6.5	1.0	1.5
Maine (ME)	10.0	10.0	10.0	10.5	11.0	11.0	11.0	11.0	11.0	10.5	10.0	9.5	1.5	2.0
Marshall Island (MH)	4.5	4.0	3.5	3.0	2.5	2.0	2.0	2.0	2.0	2.0	2.0	2.0	0.0	0.0
Maryland (MD)	8.5	9.0	9.5	9.5	9.5	9.5	9.5	10.0	10.0	9.5	9.5	9.0	3.0	3.5
Massachusetts (MA)	9.0	9.5	10.0	10.0	10.5	10.5	11.0	11.0	11.0	11.0	10.5	10.0	2.0	2.5
Mexico (MX)	4.0	3.5	3.5	3.5	3.5	4.0	4.0	4.0	4.0	4.0	4.0	4.0	0.0	0.0
Michigan (MI)	11.0	11.0	10.5	10.5	10.5	10.5	10.5	10.0	10.0	9.5	9.5	9.0	2.5	3.0
Minnesota (MN)	8.0	8.5	9.0	9.0	9.0	9.0	9.0	9.5	9.5	9.5	9.0	9.0	1.5	2.0
Mississippi (MS)	8.5	8.0	8.0	8.0	8.0	7.5	7.5	7.5	7.5	7.0	7.0	6.5	0.5	1.0
Missouri (MO)	9.0	9.5	9.5	9.5	9.5	9.5	9.5	9.0	9.0	9.0	9.0	8.5	1.5	2.0
Montana (MT)	8.5	8.0	8.0	8.0	8.0	8.0	7.5	7.5	7.5	7.5	7.0	7.0	1.5	1.5
Nebraska (NE)	11.0	10.5	10.0	10.0	10.0	10.0	10.5	11.0	11.0	11.0	10.5	10.0	1.0	1.0
Nevada (NV)	6.5	6.0	6.0	6.0	6.0	6.0	6.0	5.5	5.0	5.0	4.5	4.0	0.0	0.0
New Hampshire (NH)	8.5	8.0	8.0	8.0	8.0	8.0	8.0	8.0	8.0	8.0	7.5	7.0	0.5	0.0
New Jersey (NJ)	13.0	12.5	12.0	12.0	12.0	12.0	11.5	11.0	11.0	10.5	10.5	10.0	0.5	1.0
New Mexico (NM)	9.5	9.0	8.5	8.5	8.5	8.0	8.5	8.5	8.5	8.5	8.5	8.0	1.0	1.5
New York (NY)	12.5	13.0	13.0	13.5	14.0	14.0	14.0	14.0	14.0	14.0	14.0	13.5	1.5	2.0
North Carolina (NC)	9.5	9.5	10.0	10.0	10.0	10.0	10.0	10.0	10.0	10.0	9.5	9.0	2.5	3.0
North Dakota (ND)	8.0	7.5	7.5	7.5	7.5	7.0	7.0	7.0	7.0	7.0	6.5	6.0	0.5	1.0
Northern Marina Island (MP)	4.5	4.0	3.5	3.0	2.5	2.0	2.0	2.0	2.0	2.0	2.0	2.0	0.0	0.0
Ohio (OH)	10.5	10.5	10.5	10.5	10.5	10.5	10.5	10.5	10.5	11.0	11.0	10.5	2.0	2.0
Oklahoma (OK)	9.5	10.0	10.0	10.0	10.0	10.0	10.0	10.0	9.5	9.0	9.0	8.5	2.0	2.5
Oregon (OR)	10.5	10.0	10.0	10.0	10.0	10.0	10.0	10.0	10.5	10.5	10.5	10.0	3.5	4.0
Palau (PW)	4.5	4.0	3.5	3.0	2.5	2.0	2.0	2.0	2.0	2.0	2.0	2.0	0.0	0.0
Pennsylvania (PA)	11.5	11.0	11.0	11.0	10.5	10.5	10.5	10.5	10.0	10.0	10.0	9.5	2.0	2.5
Puerto Rico (PR)	4.5	4.0	3.5	3.0	2.5	2.0	2.0	2.0	2.0	2.0	2.0	2.0	1.0	1.0
Rhode Island (RI)	11.5	12.0	12.0	11.5	11.5	11.5	11.5	11.5	11.5	11.5	11.5	11.0	1.5	2.0
South Carolina (SC)	8.0	8.5	8.5	9.0	9.0	9.0	9.0	9.0	9.0	9.0	8.5	8.0	1.5	2.0
South Dakota (SD)	7.5	7.0	6.5	6.0	6.0	6.0	6.0	6.0	6.0	5.5	5.5	5.0	0.0	0.0
Tennessee (TN)	8.0	7.5	7.0	7.0	6.5	6.0	6.0	6.0	6.0	6.0	5.5	5.0	0.5	1.0
Texas (TX)	7.5	7.0	7.0	6.5	6.0	6.0	6.0	6.0	6.0	6.0	6.0	5.5	0.0	0.0
Utah (UT)	10.5	10.0	9.5	9.5	9.0	9.0	9.0	9.0	9.0	8.5	8.5	8.0	2.0	2.5
Vermont (VT)	10.0	10.5	10.5	10.5	10.5	10.5	10.5	10.5	10.5	10.5	10.5	10.5	1.0	1.5
Virgin Island (VI)	4.5	4.0	3.5	3.0	2.5	2.0	2.0	2.0	2.0	2.0	2.0	2.0	0.0	0.0
Virginia (VA)	8.5	9.0	9.0	9.0	9.0	9.0	9.5	9.5	9.5	9.5	9.5	9.0	2.5	3.0
Washington (WA)	10.0	9.5	9.0	8.5	8.0	8.0	7.5	7.5	7.5	7.5	7.5	7.0	0.0	0.0
West Virginia (WV)	9.5	9.0	9.0	9.0	9.0	9.0	9.0	9.0	9.0	8.5	8.0	7.5	2.0	2.5
Wisconsin (WI)	12.0	12.0	12.0	12.0	12.0	12.5	12.5	12.5	12.5	12.0	11.5	11.0	2.0	2.5
Wyoming (WY)	7.0	6.5	6.0	5.5	5.0	4.5	4.5	4.5	4.0	4.0	3.5	3.0	0.0	0.0
Not Reported (NR)	9.0	9.0	9.0	9.0	9.0	9.0	9.0	9.0	9.0	9.0	9.0	8.5	1.5	2.0

2008-2009
Institutional Methodology (IM)
Computation Tables

TABLE 2. ALLOWANCES AGAINST INCOME

FICA: Wages	
$1 to $97,500:	7.65% of income earned by each wage earner (maximum $7,458.75 per person)
$97,501 or more:	$7,458.75 + 1.45% of income earned above $97,500 by each wage earner
Elementary/secondary tuition allowance:	Reported tuition paid to per child maximum of: $7,900 based on avg. public school expenditures $6,021 based on avg. private school tuition
Employment allowance:	44% of lesser earned income to a maximum of $3,970 (single parent: 44% of earned income to a maximum of $3,970)
Medical/dental expense allowance:	Unreimbursed expenses in excess of 3.6% of total income

TABLE 3a. INCOME PROTECTION ALLOWANCE (IPA)
(Parents of Dependent Students)

Family Size* (including student)	Number in College**				
	1	2	3	4	5
2	$19,430	$18,620			
3	23,480	22,670	$21,860		
4	26,990	26,180	25,370	$24,560	
5	30,230	29,420	28,610	27,800	$26,990
6	32,930	32,120	31,310	30,500	29,690

*For each additional family member, add $2,700
**For each additional college student, subtract $810

TABLE 3b. MONTHLY MAINTENANCE ALLOWANCE
(Independent Students)

Single Student:	$1,810 per month during period of non-enrollment
Married Student:	$1,310 per month during period of non-enrollment (calculated for student and spouse)
Children of Independent Students:	$510 per month during period of non-enrollment for each child

TABLE 4. EDUCATION SAVINGS ALLOWANCES

Annual Savings Goal (ASG) =
1.52% of Total Income, to a maximum of $2,470

Annual Education Savings Allowance (AESA) =
ASG x number of pre-college children, excluding the student Applicant

Cumulative Education Savings Allowance (CESA) =
[(Number of college students x ASG x 18 x .625) +
(ASG x total ages of pre-college children)]
OR
$20,860, whichever is greater

TABLE 5. CONTRIBUTION FROM AVAILABLE INCOME (AI)
(Parents of Dependent Students)

Available Income (AI)	Total Contributions from Income				*
Less than $ 15,921		22%	of AI		22%
$ 15,921 to 21,500	$ 3,502 +	26%	of AI over	$ 15,920	26%
$ 21,501 to 27,070	$ 4,953 +	30%	of AI over	$ 21,500	30%
$ 27,071 to 32,640	$ 6,624 +	34%	of AI over	$ 27,070	34%
$ 32,641 to 38,210	$ 8,518 +	38%	of AI over	$ 32,640	38%
$ 38,211 to 43,790	$ 10,635 +	42%	of AI over	$ 38,210	42%
$ 43,791 or more	$ 12,979 +	46%	of AI over	$ 43,790	46%

*Parents' marginal rate for use in dependent student contribution from income calculation.

TABLE 6. STUDENT INCOME ASSESSMENT RATES

Independent Students ....70% of Available Income (AI)
Dependent Students ....Percentage used is based on the parents' marginal rate used in Table 5

TABLE 7. ADJUSTED NET WORTH OF A BUSINESS OR FARM

Net Worth (NW)	Adjusted Net Worth
Less than $1	$ 0
$ 1 to 110,000	$ 0 + 40% of NW
$ 110,001 to 330,000	$ 44,000 + 50% of NW over $110,000
$ 330,001 to 550,000	$ 154,000 + 60% of NW over $330,000
$ 550,001 or more	$ 286,000 + 100% of NW over $550,000

TABLE 8. EMERGENCY RESERVE ALLOWANCE (ERA)

Parents of Dependents and Independent Students with Dependents:

Family Size	ERA
2	$ 18,270
3	22,080
4	25,380
5	28,420
6	30,960
Each additional family member	+ 2,540

Single Independent Students without Dependents:	$ 1,810
Married Independent Students without Dependents:	$ 2,620

TABLE 9. ASSET CONVERSION RATE

Parents of Dependent Students

Discretionary Net Worth	Total Contribution From Assets
Up to $ 30,960	3%
30,961 to 61,920	930 + 4% of DNW over $ 30,960
61,921 or more	$2,170 + 5% of DNW over $ 61,920

All Students:
Asset conversion rate is 25% of discretionary net worth

TABLE 10. NUMBER IN COLLEGE ADJUSTMENT

Number of Children In College	Adjustment Rate
1	100% of PC
2	60%
3	45%
4+	35%

For independent students, the adjustment rate is determined by the total Number of children, including the student, spouse, and dependent children.

TABLE 11. STUDENT STANDARD CONTRIBUTION
FROM INCOME

$ 1,550 .... Freshman Dependent Students
2,150 .... All Other Dependent Students
2,950 .... All Independent Students

2007–2008 Estimated Parents' Contribution (IM)

Net Assets:	$25,000				$50,000		
Family Size:	3	4	5	6	3	4	5
2006 income before taxes:							
$10,000	$0	$0	$0	$0	$0	$0	$0
$15,000	$0	$0	$0	$0	$0	$0	$0
$20,000	$0	$0	$0	$0	$0	$0	$0
$25,000	$0	$0	$0	$0	$87	$0	$0
$30,000	$0	$0	$0	$0	$197	$0	$0
$35,000	$225	$0	$0	$0	$501	$104	$0
$40,000	$980	$209	$0	$0	$1,256	$391	$0
$45,000	$1,732	$945	$214	$0	$2,008	$1,126	$214
$50,000	$2,484	$1,680	$933	$300	$2,760	$1,853	$933
$55,000	$3,236	$2,415	$1,651	$1,002	$3,512	$2,529	$1,651
$60,000	$4,092	$3,150	$2,370	$1,704	$4,368	$3,204	$2,370
$65,000	$5,003	$3,971	$3,088	$2,405	$5,279	$3,971	$3,088
$70,000	$6,028	$4,840	$3,878	$3,107	$6,304	$4,840	$3,878
$75,000	$7,132	$5,843	$4,727	$3,880	$7,408	$5,843	$4,727
$80,000	$8,294	$6,896	$5,690	$4,710	$8,570	$6,896	$5,690
$85,000	$9,458	$8,025	$6,697	$5,647	$9,734	$8,025	$6,697
$90,000	$10,586	$9,072	$7,743	$6,623	$10,862	$9,072	$7,743
$95,000	$11,832	$10,170	$8,746	$7,602	$12,108	$10,170	$8,746
$100,000	$13,238	$11,472	$9,915	$8,659	$13,514	$11,472	$9,915

Note: The figures shown are parents' contribution under Institutional Methodology (IM) with both parents employed (equal wages). Income is only from employment, taking standard deductions on U.S. income tax and filing a joint 1040 tax return. The contribution levels calculated are for one undergraduate child enrolled in college. In the household size of 4, the younger sibling is age 15. In the household size of 5, the younger siblings are ages 15 and 13. In the household size of 6, the younger siblings are ages 15, 13, and 11.

	$100,000				$150,000			
6	3	4	5	6	3	4	5	6
$0	$1,341	$1,073	$839	$684	$3,653	$3,319	$3,009	$2,749
$0	$1,507	$1,237	$985	$802	$3,862	$3,523	$3,209	$2,946
$0	$1,674	$1,400	$1,146	$933	$4,070	$3,728	$3,410	$3,143
$0	$1,822	$1,558	$1,307	$1,090	$4,254	$3,925	$3,611	$3,340
$0	$1,968	$1,702	$1,455	$1,119	$4,438	$4,104	$3,796	$3,376
$0	$2,295	$1,845	$1,548	$1,104	$4,795	$4,284	$3,912	$3,358
$0	$3,050	$2,157	$1,569	$1,089	$5,550	$4,622	$3,939	$3,339
$0	$3,802	$2,893	$1,759	$1,074	$6,302	$5,357	$4,123	$3,320
$300	$4,554	$3,617	$2,358	$1,295	$7,054	$6,079	$4,692	$3,521
$1,002	$5,306	$4,273	$2,957	$1,854	$7,806	$6,715	$5,262	$4,032
$1,704	$6,162	$4,928	$3,557	$2,441	$8,662	$7,350	$5,831	$4,542
$2,405	$7,073	$5,669	$4,156	$3,028	$9,573	$8,071	$6,400	$5,053
$3,107	$8,098	$6,459	$4,826	$3,615	$10,598	$8,841	$7,041	$5,564
$3,880	$9,202	$7,381	$5,569	$4,274	$11,702	$9,744	$7,741	$6,146
$4,710	$10,364	$8,355	$6,443	$4,989	$12,864	$10,697	$8,555	$6,785
$5,647	$11,528	$9,404	$7,360	$5,812	$14,028	$11,727	$9,413	$7,573
$6,623	$12,656	$10,371	$8,317	$6,673	$15,156	$12,673	$10,309	$8,395
$7,602	$13,902	$11,390	$9,230	$7,602	$16,402	$13,672	$11,163	$9,222
$8,659	$15,308	$12,612	$10,309	$8,659	$17,808	$14,874	$12,183	$10,125

Source: The College Board. The College Board is a national nonprofit association that champions educational excellence for all students through the ongoing collaboration of nearly 5,200 member schools, colleges, universities, education systems, organizations, and agencies.

5 What Do We Need to Do, and When?

Now that you have an idea of the college costs your family faces, the kinds of financing options available, and how your family's financial situation will be viewed by the others in the partnership, you'll want to know how to make sure you apply for funding in a timely way.

Don't forget to meet the deadlines for admissions application materials, too. The most accurate and timely financial aid applications will be of no use if your child does not meet admissions deadlines!

Unless you look forward to filling out your income tax forms every year, you probably won't find filling out financial aid forms much fun. But the potential payoff for your child should help see you through the process. And you'll only have to fill out the FAFSA, and CSS/Financial Aid PROFILE if it is used by your child's college choices, once each year. Information on the FAFSA and PROFILE will be sent to all the colleges your child lists on the forms as possible college choices.

A note about Early Decision and Early Action admissions programs: If your child is applying to his or her first-choice college under one of these early plans, it is especially important to find out from the college what the deadlines for aid consideration are. Often you have to complete aid forms before you have the benefit of official income tax information; you simply estimate as accurately as you can what your financial situation will be by the end of the tax year. The college will use this estimated information to determine any financial aid package, which will be altered, if necessary, after your year-end information has been reported on the FAFSA or other required forms.

The early bird gets the worm.

Actually, it's not so much that the early bird gets the worm as the late bird gets little or nothing. While it is critical to adhere to the priority deadlines established by each college for its financial aid application process, sending in hurriedly completed information—or a FAFSA before January 1—may well delay you in the process while inaccuracies are corrected or numbers adjusted. Perhaps you should revise this thinking to "the timely bird gets the worm."

A General Calendar for Completing the Financial Aid Application Process

While the very best source of information about the forms you'll need to file—and when you will need to file them—will be the financial aid offices at the colleges to which your child is applying, it is important to understand the general sequence of the financial aid application process. It is outlined below.

1. No later than fall of the senior year of high school, your child should gather admissions and financial aid information from colleges of interest. Determine which financial aid application forms your family will be required to file to qualify for aid, and get copies of the forms.

➡ The FAFSA will be available in the late fall in your high school guidance office or from the financial aid office at colleges. The FAFSA on the Web is available after January 1, 2008: www.fafsa.ed.gov.

➡ The CSS/Financial Aid PROFILE Registration and Application Guide will be available in the early fall in your child's high school guidance office or from colleges using the service. The registration guide assists students in completing the online application.

➡ College financial aid forms, when required, will be available directly from the college and are often included in the admissions application materials.

2. If applying to one or more colleges that use PROFILE, register for your customized application at www.collegeboard.com. Registrations are accepted beginning October 1 of the year prior to your child's intended college enrollment. Once you register through collegeboard.com, you will be given an option to complete your application immediately or to return to the application at a later time.

3. The PROFILE offers a customized preapplication worksheet and instructions in both English and Spanish. This form can be printed from the Web site after the registration step and reviewed with parents prior to completing the remainder of online applications.

4. Complete the PROFILE, if required, and submit the form in time for the College Board to receive it by your earliest college-specified financial aid deadline. In general, it is recommended that you complete the PROFILE at least two weeks in advance of the college's deadline.

5. Complete the FAFSA after January 1 of the college enrollment year, but at least four weeks before the earliest financial aid deadline set by the college or state scholarship or grant programs to which your child is applying, or complete FAFSA on the Web at www.fafsa.ed.gov.

6. Complete and return any other required financial aid application forms.

7. Within two weeks of submitting the FAFSA through the mail, your child will receive from the U.S. Department of Education his or her Student Aid Report (SAR), which includes the federal government's determination of your expected family contribution and lists the information you reported on the FAFSA. If you file the FAFSA online, you can view and print the SAR within several days of filing. If you find any errors, be sure to correct them and return the form right away to the federal processing center so that the corrected information can be sent to the colleges where your child is applying.

8.   Once the PROFILE Application has been submitted, your child will receive an online PROFILE Acknowledgment containing the following information:

➡   The Acknowledgment confirms the colleges and programs that will be receiving the PROFILE information.

➡   The Data Confirmation section of the Acknowledgment provides a record of the information the family submitted for PROFILE processing and reporting. Applicants may print this form, make needed corrections, and mail it directly to the applicant's schools.

When you fill out financial aid application forms, you will want to be as complete and accurate as you can about indicating your financial circumstances. If you omit requested information, or use different figures for such items as income or savings on different aid application forms, the extra time needed to supply the correct information will delay your child's application.

It's so complicated, we'll have to hire a financial adviser.

While the financial aid application process can be time-consuming, it generally becomes complicated only if you and your child don't allow enough time to find out what's required and then do it. If you read this book as well as information from your child's college choices carefully, you should have in hand what you need to complete the process successfully. The instructions that accompany both the FAFSA and the CSS/Financial Aid PROFILE are detailed and comprehensive.

For more assistance keeping on top of financial aid deadlines, use the "My Organizer" link on the collegeboard.com Web site.

 For more information on the application process:

College admissions and financial aid offices

College Board on the Web: www.collegeboard.com

College and university Web sites

FAFSA on the Web: www.fafsa.ed.gov

High school counselors

 Questions Families Should Ask About What They Need to Do, and When

Financial aid administrators at the colleges your child is considering will be able to give you the answers to these questions. The worksheet on page 70 will help you keep track of the dates required materials are due—and keep you on track during the financial aid application process.

1. What financial aid forms are required by this college? How can we obtain copies of these forms? Can we get assistance from the college in completing the forms?

2. When are the forms due to be completed and returned to the processor and/or college? If we miss the deadline, will we still be considered for aid?

3. Will a copy of parents' and/or students' tax forms be required? If so, by when?

4. When will we receive notification of the college's financial aid decision?

5. What is the deadline for accepting the financial aid award?

6. Are other documents required before the financial aid award can be finalized?

Worksheet 4: Tracking Your Financial Aid Application Requirements

	Required Forms Deadline	Due Date/ Completed	Date
Institution _____			
FAFSA	____	____	____
PROFILE			
• Registration	____	____	____
• Application	____	____	____
College Forms	____	____	____
Tax Forms	____	____	____
Other	____	____	____
Institution _____			
FAFSA	____	____	____
PROFILE			
• Registration	____	____	____
• Application	____	____	____
College Forms	____	____	____
Tax Forms	____	____	____
Other	____	____	____
Institution _____			
FAFSA	____	____	____
PROFILE			
• Registration	____	____	____
• Application	____	____	____
College Forms	____	____	____
Tax Forms	____	____	____
Other	____	____	____
Institution _____			
FAFSA	____	____	____
PROFILE			
• Registration	____	____	____
• Application	____	____	____
College Forms	____	____	____
Tax Forms	____	____	____
Other	____	____	____

Be sure to submit required admissions applications on time as well. Financial aid decisions are not made until a student is accepted for admission.

6 $ What Does This Aid Package REALLY Mean?

If you and your child have followed the admissions and financial aid application timelines for the colleges to which he or she decided to apply—and your child was realistic about the likelihood of admission—chances are there will be more than one "fat envelope" arriving in your mailbox in the spring of senior year. If your circumstances warrant it, these acceptance materials will include a financial aid award.

Many families are surprised each year to find differences—sometimes quite significant ones—between the financial aid awards offered by different colleges, even when college costs are similar. These families think they know what their "need" will be, and expect that financial aid from each school will include a similar plan for covering the difference between the cost of attendance and the expected family contribution.

But, having read this far, you realize that Institutional Methodology is not a strict formula that all colleges use to determine need (as compared with Federal Methodology, which determines eligibility for federal funds). And there is no specific formula governing how all the colleges will "package" the financial aid that students and families are offered. There is, however, likely to be a formula that each *individual* college has developed to award its limited financial aid resources.

When you find differences in calculated need and in the terms of financial aid awarded, you can be sure the professional judgment of the college's financial aid administrator came into play. Based on their experience with other families in similar circumstances, financial aid administrators may use their own judgment to interpret a family's financial data differently than the standard methodology might suggest. Examples of some of the variations within IM might include the calculation of a contribution from the noncustodial parent, or limiting the impact of home equity by capping the home value at a certain level. In addition, some schools impute asset values based on reported interest and dividends, or choose to allow expenses for private elementary or secondary school tuition to be factored into their decision on a family's ability to pay for college. Adjustments to IM can affect the final determination of eligibility for institutional funding.

A financial aid package is the total financial aid award received by a student; it may be made up of a combination of aid that includes both gift aid and self-help. Because it is likely that the financial aid packages your child receives will be at least slightly different, it will be important for you to get them all in hand and review them with some key criteria in mind. You'll want to compare apples to apples insofar as you are able. For example, a total aid package of $20,000 may seem on the face of it to be preferable to one totaling $15,000. But you'll need to compare the actual components of the packages to determine which is better for you and your child in the long run.

Factors to Consider in Comparing Offers
Percentage of Grant Aid Versus Loan Aid

In general, the higher the proportion of grant aid versus loan aid, the more attractive the package will be in the long term. Students will have fewer debts to repay and the cost of attending college will be lower. More attractive packages are often offered to students in whom colleges are most interested. In fact, some colleges will offer a package of near-total grant aid for the students they most want to come to their campuses.

Percentage of Self-Help Versus Grant Aid

This is a broader way of comparing aid packages than by looking strictly at grant versus loan. Self-help includes not only the expected family contribution and the loans that are offered in the aid package but also any student employment monies that are included. While there may well be advantages to working on campus beyond financial ones, some families feel that an aid package that does not include the expectation that the student work during the academic year is preferable to one that does. You'll also want to compare the colleges' expectations for summer earnings and be realistic about whether your child will be able to earn what each college is expecting.

Terms of Loans

Student loans based on financial need, with low interest rates and no expected payments until after the student graduates or leaves college, are preferable to unsubsidized loans or loans your child might be recommended to take out from private lending sources.

Gapping

This term refers to the process by which a "gap" is left unfilled in the aid package between the cost of attendance and the family's expected contribution. If your child has been "gapped" at a particular college, it means that your family would be expected to find this money somewhere else if your child were to enroll. It is important to compare the proportion of unmet need (or gap), if any, in evaluating financial aid award packages.

While you are involved in interpreting and comparing your child's financial aid awards, be sure to keep in mind the deadlines set by the colleges for acceptance of awards. If you miss the deadline, your child's financial aid package could be offered to another student. You should also bear in mind that your child is not required to accept the entire aid package as offered. But if he or she does decline a part of it, such as the work-study opportunity, the college may not be able to restore that aid if your child changes his or her mind later.

Aid Renewal

If your child has been awarded a scholarship, whether based on financial need or academic merit, it will be important to know whether the scholarship is renewable in subsequent years and, if so, under what conditions. If the institution's renewal policies are unclear in the materials accompanying the aid offer, do not hesitate to ask the financial aid office.

You don't need to let yourself be pressured into making an immediate decision about whether to accept an aid offer. If necessary, contact the financial aid office and request an extension of the deadline. (For information on what to do if you believe the financial aid package offered will not provide enough assistance, see Chapter 7.)

The case studies that follow will give you an idea of the amount of variation you might find in your child's financial aid packages and provide clues for interpreting various awards. The worksheet at the end of this chapter provides a tool for comparing apples to apples once your child receives his or her financial aid offers. An interactive, online version of this worksheet, Compare Your Financial Aid Awards, is available through College Board on the Web at www.collegeboard.com.

Comparing Financial Aid Packages

Sarah Smith

	(FM) Prairie	(FM) Old Bricks	(FM) Central
Cost of Attendance	**$14,400**	**$32,000**	**$31,000**
Family Contribution	4,664	4,664	4,664
Contribution from Noncustodial Parent	—	3,000	—
Outside Scholarship	1,000	1,000	1,000
Financial Need	**$8,736**	**$23,336**	**$25,336**
Financial Aid Packages			
Federal Pell Grant	$ 0	$ 0	$ 0
State Scholarship Grant	2,000	2,000	2,000
Institutional Grant	0	15,000	11,000
Federal Perkins Loan	1,500	1,000	0
Federal Stafford or Direct Loan	3,500	3,500	3,500
Federal Work-Study	1,700	1,800	1,500
TOTAL AWARD	**$8,700**	**$23,300**	**$18,000**

*Board only since student will live at home

When comparing the financial aid packages Sarah received, she and her mother noted four key points to consider:

➡️ *Noncustodial parent contribution:* Old Bricks was the only college to require Sarah's father to provide financial information on the College Board's Noncustodial PROFILE Application. The financial aid office there is expecting him to contribute $3,000 toward Sarah's freshman-year cost of attendance. The other colleges do not have this same expectation. This is one of the areas where colleges have the option to customize their aid policies to ensure that they are awarding limited institutional grant aid to the neediest applicants. These colleges believe that both of the student's birth or adoptive parents have the responsibility to pay for the student's education, to the extent they are able. In making a final decision about where to attend, this is a factor Sarah and her mother will need to consider.

➡️ *Whether need is met:* Old Bricks and Prairie have offered Sarah aid packages that virtually meet her demonstrated need. Central has offered a package that leaves over $7,000 of her need unmet; there is a "gap" between the aid award and her financial need. Some institutions meet full need and others do not; it is an institutional decision, based in large part on the financial aid budget at the college. Sarah and her mother will need to take this into consideration and find another source of funding to cover the gap should Sarah decide to enroll at Central.

➡️ *Loan expectations:* Central expects that Sarah will borrow from one loan program; Old Bricks and Prairie include two loans in the package, although the total borrowing requirement is similar at these institutions. Borrowing from both the Perkins and Stafford Loan Programs could mean two separate repayment obligations after graduation, unless Sarah applies to consolidate them. This is another factor for Sarah and her mother to consider, in light of what her earning potential may be after college and how much of a debt burden she can realistically carry.

➡️ *Outside scholarship:* Sarah was awarded a Rotary Club Scholarship of $1,000. Old Bricks reduced her Federal Perkins Loan from $2,000 to $1,000 to recognize her award. Both Prairie and Central reduced her Institutional Grant by $1,000*. Since the Rotary Club Scholarship is for only one year, it will be important for Sarah to understand how her financial aid package will change at each school in subsequent years. Will Prairie and Central increase her grant by $1,000? Will Old Bricks increase her Perkins Loan?

*This resulted in no institutional grant from Prairie.

James Washington

	Colony	Very Old Bricks	Division
Cost of Attendance	$19,900	$49,100	$37,200
Family Contribution	(FM) 14,949	*(IM) 11,085	(IM) 11,595
Financial Need	$4,951	$38,015	$25,605
Financial Aid Packages			
Federal Pell Grant	$ 0	$ 0	$ 0
State Scholarship Grant	1,200	1,200	1,200
Institutional Grant	0	31,300	16,400
Private Scholarship	0	0	0
Federal Perkins Loan	0	0	2,500
Federal Stafford or			
Direct Loan	3,500	3,500	3,500
Federal Work-Study		2,000	2,000
TOTAL AWARD	**$4,700**	**$38,000**	**$25,600**

* Very Old Bricks uses IM with options to determine the family contribution. In this example, they have allowed an additional cost of living allowance adjustment for James's family because they live in Boston.

These are the key points James and his family are considering in comparing the financial aid offers he received:

➡ *Family contribution:* Colony used Federal Methodology in determining James's financial need, whereas Very Old Bricks and Division used Institutional Methodology. The family contribution expected from Very Old Bricks and Division takes into consideration the substantial unreimbursed medical expenses incurred by James's family, and recognizes the need for James's parents to save for his sister's college education. In addition, Very Old Bricks uses IM with an allowance for higher cost of living expenses in Boston, resulting in a lower family contribution. This illustrates how Institutional Methodology can be more sensitive than Federal Methodology to individual family circumstances. James and his family may want to appeal the aid decision at Colony, documenting the high medical expenses that were not taken into account in the FM analysis.

Grants and the big picture: At first glance, the total cost of attendance at Very Old Bricks looks dramatically higher than that of the other two schools. But Very Old Bricks has offered James a very large grant that makes the net cost of attendance very affordable.

Cost of attendance: Even though Colony has offered James only a state grant and a small loan, it may turn out to be the most realistic choice from a purely financial point of view. The cost of attendance for Colony is less than that at Very Old Bricks or at Division; and the double loan expectation requirements built into the Division package make it more costly in the long run. James's family might be able to finance the family contribution at Colony in such a way that it makes little impact on their current income and lifestyle.

Maria Martinez

	Canyon	Major Mortar	Midway
Cost of Attendance	**$9,500**	**$46,600**	**$33,300**
Family Contribution	(FM) 23,668	(IM) 23,657	(IM) 23,657
Outside Scholarship	3,000	3,000	3,000
Financial Need	**$ 0**	**$19,943**	**$6,643**
Financial Aid Packages			
Federal Pell Grant	$ 0	$ 0	$ 0
State Scholarship Grant	0	0	0
Institutional Grant	0	14,900	1,900
Federal Perkins Loan	0	0	0
Federal Stafford Loan or Direct Loan	0	3,500	3,500
Federal Work-Study	0	1,500	1,200
TOTAL AWARD	**$ 0**	**$19,900**	**$6,600**

Other financing alternatives not based on financial need or student merit suggested by Maria's college choices:

	Canyon	Major Mortar	Midway
Federal PLUS Loan (Up to cost of attendance minus financial aid)	yes	yes	yes
Institutional Payment Plan	no	yes	yes
Institutional Loan (to replace family contribution)	no	yes	no
Home Equity Line of Credit	yes	yes	yes

Given what Maria and her parents had estimated their expected family contribution would be, they are not surprised by the financial aid they have been offered by the colleges to which she was admitted. However, there are some key factors for consideration as Maria makes her college choice:

➡ *Cost of attendance/private scholarship:* The outside scholarship Maria received from an organization supporting Hispanic women majoring in the sciences makes a more dramatic difference at Canyon, her least expensive option (where it cuts her costs almost in half) than it does at the other two colleges. (Maria might also want to find out if the—currently need-based—athletic scholarship she has been offered from Major Mortar would increase in future years if she excels on the college tennis team.)

➡ *Financing alternatives:* Maria's parents will want to look into a variety of options for financing college costs. The institutional payment plans offered at Major Mortar and Midway would help them spread the costs over the calendar year, rather than the two lump-sum semester payments required at Canyon. Major Mortar also sponsors an institutional loan program that might offer generous terms. If Maria is seriously considering Major Mortar or Midway, it's likely her parents will investigate a Federal PLUS Loan or establish a line of credit based on their home equity.

If it can sometimes be difficult to justify the differences in the financial aid packages your child receives, it is even more problematic to try to compare the aid your child receives with what the student down the street received. It's not uncommon for parents to complain that "John Doe, whose parents are in the same income bracket, received more aid than my child." By now you realize that a lot of other factors may well have been involved. You'll do best to save your energy and devote it to ensuring that your child makes the most of the financial aid opportunities afforded him or her.

For more information on comparing award offers:

Admissions and financial aid offices at the colleges where your child was admitted

Guide to Getting Financial Aid 2008

College Board on the Web: www.collegeboard.com

High school counselor

Questions Families Should Ask Colleges About the Aid Package

Many colleges provide a helpful enclosure with financial aid awards, explaining the college's financial aid packaging philosophy and the factors that went into determining the family's expected contribution and financial need. Such enclosures often include detailed information about facets of the aid package such as loan terms and sources. If you don't find such information accompanying a college's financial aid award, you may want to ask the financial aid office some of the following questions.

1. What are the terms (interest, repayment policies) of the loans that are part of this aid package?

2. How likely are we to qualify for the parent loans that are part of this package?

3. What if my child decides he or she would like to work outside the work-study job included in this aid package?

4. If my child declines the work or loan portion of this aid package, what are the chances of getting a work-study job or loan later if my child changes his or her mind?

5. What are recommended sources of additional funding to cover the gap (if any) between what our family can afford and what the aid package covers?

6. Is it possible to get an extension of the financial aid acceptance deadline to more thoroughly compare the aid awards my child has received?

7. How will any outside scholarships my child might be awarded after accepting this offer affect the aid package?

8. If our family financial situation remains about the same, how will grant and loan amounts change during the years my child is enrolled?

9. How often will my child be paid for hours worked through the work-study program? Will my child receive pay checks or will the earnings be applied to my child's bank account?

Worksheet 5: Comparing Award Letters

STEP 1 List the name of each school you want to consider attending, the award deadline date, and the total cost of attendance (see Chapter 2). This information should be in your award letter. If not, refer to the college catalog to estimate the cost of attendance, or call the financial aid office.

	College 1	College 2	College 3	College 4
Name of College	_____	_____	_____	_____
Award Deadline Date	_____	_____	_____	_____
Total Cost of Attendance	$_____	$_____	$_____	$_____

STEP 2 List the financial aid awards each school is offering. Don't forget that grants, scholarships, and work-study *do not* have to be repaid, while all loans *must* be repaid.

Grants and Scholarships

	College 1	College 2	College 3	College 4
Federal Pell	$_____	$_____	$_____	$_____
Federal SEOG	$_____	$_____	$_____	$_____
State	$_____	$_____	$_____	$_____
College	$_____	$_____	$_____	$_____
Other	$_____	$_____	$_____	$_____
TOTAL Grants and Scholarships	$_____	$_____	$_____	$_____
Percentage of package that is grant	_____%	_____%	_____%	_____%

Work-Study Opportunities

	College 1	College 2	College 3	College 4
	$_____	$_____	$_____	$_____

Loans

	College 1	College 2	College 3	College 4
Federal Stafford-Direct	$_____	$_____	$_____	$_____
Federal Perkins	$_____	$_____	$_____	$_____
Other	$_____	$_____	$_____	$_____
TOTAL Loans	$_____	$_____	$_____	$_____
Percentage of package that is work or loans	_____%	_____%	_____%	_____%

Worksheet 5:
Continued

Total Financial Aid Award

Grants and Scholarships+
Work-Study + Loans = $_____ $_____ $_____ $_____

STEP 3 Calculate what it will cost you to attend the college you are considering. For each college, enter the total cost of attendance. Then, subtract the total financial aid award from the total cost of attendance. That number is the net cost, or what it will cost you to attend that school.

A. Total Cost of Attendance

$_____ $_____ $_____ $_____

B. Total Financial Aid Award

$_____ $_____ $_____ $_____

C. Net Cost to Attend
    (A minus B = C) $_____ $_____ $_____ $_____

What Do We Do If the Aid Package Is Not Enough?

After careful review of the financial aid packages your child receives, you may be convinced that the contribution expected of your family is not at all realistic. You may decide that further follow-up is warranted with your child's first-choice college to see if other arrangements might be made to help you meet college costs. Before doing this, however, you should be aware that the majority of colleges have limited funds and a strict campus policy for awarding them, as well as a written policy about adjustments that can be made to the family contribution.

Appeal Strategies

If you decide to appeal the financial aid award your child has received, you will first need to contact the college financial aid office to find out what process, if any, they employ in reviewing financial aid awards. At this point, you should be prepared to discuss any special circumstances that may have been overlooked. Most financial aid administrators will request that special circumstances or changes in income or other data that have occurred since the time of your application for aid be put in writing, even if they are willing to discuss the situation by phone first. Whatever the case, be sure to follow the college's guidelines for appealing an award, so that you will not delay the process.

Be sure that you have data, not just emotion, to back up your concerns about how much the college is expecting you to pay. Few aid officers are impressed by unsubstantiated whining!

If you are able to provide substantive new information, or a valuable reinterpretation of old data, it is possible that the financial aid administrator may be able to adjust your child's award to make meeting college costs more feasible. You'll need to bear in mind that financial aid officers must constantly prioritize the needs of the many families who ask for assistance. Even if you have a demonstrated need for additional aid, there may be other families with greater needs who must be served.

Most colleges will bargain with families about the aid decision.

While many colleges will listen to an informed and data-based appeal, it is not true that most colleges will bargain. Although there are some exceptions, most financial aid officers are governed by strict campus policies that attempt to ensure equitable awards for all deserving applicants. They can, of course, use their professional judgment to make warranted adjustments in a package that was put together without knowledge of special circumstances. But you should not approach the comparison of your award packages as the basis for "let's make a deal" negotiations.

Other Financing Options

There are two categories of families who are likely to find alternative funding sources attractive:

➡ those who demonstrate no financial need but are looking for ways to reduce the impact of college costs on their day-to-day lifestyle

➡ those who are not completely satisfied with the amount of aid available to them through the college's financial aid package

In either case, there are a variety of options to consider. Details about these programs can be found in Chapter 3.

Unsubsidized Federal Loans

These student loans are administered by participating colleges (Federal Direct Loans) or available from a lending institution (Federal Family Educational Loans/Stafford).

Federal PLUS Loans (Parent)

You can borrow any amount between the cost of attendance and any aid your child has already received.

Privately Funded Student and Parent Loans

There are a variety of commercial sources for loans that are not based on need but on ability to repay and credit history.

Student Employment

Even if your child does not qualify for a need-based job, he or she may be able to get a job on campus or a part-time job off campus. For most students, the days of being able to work one's way through college are over, but part-time work can help meet some of the costs for personal expenses or books.

When your child looks for a part-time job, it is important to keep in mind that campus employers are likely to be more flexible than off-campus employers about work hours during exam weeks and vacation periods.

Tuition Payment Plans

These plans fall into two general categories:

➡ those that allow parents to spread payment of college costs throughout the year

➡ prepayment plans, for those who can afford the total four-year cost in advance to avoid any future inflation-related increases

Some tuition payment plans are college based, while others are commercial plans that may be recommended by the college.

Qualified State Tuition Programs

Many states have begun investment programs to help residents save for future college expenses. State-sponsored 529 plans, as they are frequently called, allow families to save tax deferred until the money is withdrawn for payment of a child's college expenses, at which point it is taxed at the child's rate.

There are two types of Qualified State Tuition Programs: a prepaid tuition plan and a college savings plan. The prepaid tuition plan enables families to lock in future tuition at today's rates, based on state school costs. The more popular college savings plans normally offer more attractive investment options. Unlike the Coverdell Education Savings Accounts, the 529 savings plans have no income limits to participate and allow much larger annual contributions.

All 50 states and the District of Columbia have implemented either a college savings plan, or a prepaid tuition program. Check with your appropriate state agency to learn more about the program available where you live. A complete list of these programs is included in the Appendix.

Coverdell Education Savings and Higher Education Expenses

The Coverdell ESA is a method of saving for future college costs. Virtually any-one—parents, grandparents, or even family friends—can open an Education Savings Account for a child under 18 years of age. Contributions are not tax deductible in the year they are made, but account earnings will be deferred from federal income tax until withdrawn. Upon withdrawal, both contributions and account earnings are free of federal tax if they are used for tuition fees, room and board, and books and supplies at a qualified college or vocational school. Annual contributions of up to $2,000 may be made to an ESA if the person funding the account has a modified adjusted gross income of less than $110,000 for a single tax filer or $220,000 for joint filers.

Some colleges permit families to use a credit card for tuition payments. This permits families to accumulate benefits (such as airline or hotel points) through their affinity credit cards, which may make payment a little less painful. Consider using those airline points to pay for your child's trip home at the end of the year!

Comparison of No-Need Loans

Unsubsidized Federal Stafford Loans

Advantages	Disadvantages
• Loans are guaranteed by federal government • Lowest interest rate (and cap) of any education loan • Six-month grace period and graduated repayment option • No credit criteria • Loans can be consolidated • Forbearance and deferments available • Cancellation provisions same as other Title IV program • Flexible repayment terms and borrower benefits from some lenders	• Student responsible for paying interest during in-school grace and deferment periods (though it may be capitalized) • 1.5% origination fee is charged and deducted from loan proceeds • Insurance premium of up to 1% may be charged by guaranty agency • Shifts debt burden to dependent student and away from parent

PLUS

Advantages	Disadvantages
• Loans are guaranteed by federal government • Borrower cannot have adverse credit as defined by the Department of Education (ED) • Borrowers of all income levels can apply • Loans can be consolidated • Cancellation provisions • Forbearance available, some deferments • Flexible repayment available from some lenders	• Without annual or aggregate borrowing maximums, borrowers must be very careful not to borrow more than they can repay • 3% origination fee is charged and deducted from proceeds • Though minimum credit standards are set by ED, lenders' policies may vary in credit review • In-school deferments available for graduate student borrowers; in most cases, parent borrowers go into repayment after full disbursement of loan • Insurance premium of up to 1% may be charged by guaranty agency.

Alternative Loans

Advantages	Disadvantages
• Generally there is no collateral required • Many loans have home equity option • Parents are limited to borrowing what they can afford to repay—responsible debt is incurred • School deferments available with some lenders • May be financially competitive with PLUS depending on APR	• A "clean" credit record and acceptable debt to income ratio (normally 38–40%) are usually required to qualify • No cancellation provisions unless parent/borrower purchases such an option • Limits on amounts that parents and students can borrow with some lenders

Home Equity Loans

Advantages	Disadvantages
• Interest is tax deductible if borrower itemizes deductions on tax return	• There may be fees (title search, appraisal) associated with obtaining the loan • Accumulating all the paperwork and processing the loan can take as long as three months, depending on the lender's volume • The family home is put up for long-term debt at a time when many people, facing retirement, want their home debt free

Student and Parent Loans

Name and Sponsor	Maximum Amount	Credit Requirements	Interest Rate	Maximum Term	Fees	Principal Deferral
Subsidized Stafford Loan (student loan)	1st-year students: $3,500; 2nd year: $4,500; 3rd–5th year: $5,500	None	Fixed at 6.8%	10 years	0–2.5%	Yes
Unsubsidized Stafford Loan (student loan)	1st-year students: $3,500; 2nd year: $4,500; 3rd–5th year: $5,500 Additional amounts for independent students: 1st-and 2nd-year students: $4,000 3rd–5th year: $5,000	None	Fixed at 6.8%	10 years	0–2.5%	Yes
PLUS	Cost of education minus financial aid	No current loan delinquencies of 90 days or longer	Fixed at 8.5%	10 years	3–4%	Yes–grad student borrower No–parent borrower

*Check with your financial aid office for information about other alternative loans.

Calculating Your Monthly Loan Payment

This chart illustrates repayment over 10 years for various loan amounts and interest rates. To calculate a monthly payment for a loan amount other than those on the chart, multiply the amount borrowed by the repayment factor for your interest rate. For example, if you borrowed $12,500 at 7.5 percent, your monthly payment would be $148.46 ($12,500 x .0118770).

Amount of Loan	Interest Rate	Repayment Factor	Monthly Payment
$10,000	4.00%	.010125	$101.25
	4.50%	.010364	$103.64
	5.00%	.010607	$106.07
	5.50%	.010853	$108.53
	6.00%	.011102	$111.02
	6.50%	.011355	$113.55
	7.00%	.011611	$116.11
	7.50%	.011870	$118.70
	8.00%	.012133	$121.33
	8.50%	.012399	$123.99
	9.00%	.012668	$126.68
$20,000	4.00%	.010125	$202.50
	4.50%	.010364	$207.28
	5.00%	.010607	$212.14
	5.50%	.010853	$217.06
	6.00%	.011102	$222.04
	6.50%	.011355	$227.10
	7.00%	.011611	$232.22
	7.50%	.011870	$237.40
	8.00%	.012133	$242.66
	8.50%	.012399	$247.98
	9.00%	.012668	$253.36
$30,000	4.00%	.010125	$303.75
	4.50%	.010364	$310.92
	5.00%	.010607	$318.20
	5.50%	.010853	$325.59
	6.00%	.011102	$333.06
	6.50%	.011355	$340.65
	7.00%	.011611	$348.33
	7.50%	.011870	$356.10
	8.00%	.012133	$363.99
	8.50%	.012399	$371.97
	9.00%	.012668	$380.04

For more information on other financing resources:

College Board on the Web: www.collegeboard.com

Guide to Getting Financial Aid 2008

College financial aid and business offices

Questions Families Should Ask Colleges When the Aid
Package Is Not Enough

If there is a significant discrepancy between what you believe your family
can afford and what the college has offered as a financial aid package, you
may want to contact the college financial aid office to ask the following questions:

1.   Is it possible to appeal this financial aid package?

2.   What are the criteria for making an appeal?

3.   What procedures should we follow in making an appeal, and
     when will we hear the results?

4.   What alternative funding sources would you recommend?

5.   What financing plans are available?

Worksheet 6: Debt Planning for Borrowers from Federal PLUS and Private Supplemental Loan Programs

Some parents elect to borrow from private loan programs, sometimes called "supplemental" or "alternative" loan programs. Most of these programs make loans on the basis of the applicant's credit history and debt-to-income ratio. The criteria for determining whether an applicant is creditworthy are more stringent in private loan programs than in the Federal PLUS program.

The worksheet on page 93 explains the credit history review process and will help you determine your debt-to-income ratio.

Your Credit History

In preparing to pay for college, you should maintain a good credit history that complies with industry standards. Check your credit history periodically to ensure that your records are accurate and up to date. Errors and inconsistencies can occur, particularly when a person's name or address changes. Resolve any problems as soon as you identify them. You may wish to check with your lender before you submit an application to determine whether there are any particular criteria (beyond the industry standards) that you will need to meet.

Some lenders also allow you to be preapproved for a loan. This means that the lender will check your credit history and let you know if you are eligible for the loan. You then submit an application to complete the loan process.

Your Debt-to-Income Ratio

Calculating your debt-to-income ratio is one way that a lender determines how much *additional* debt you can handle, based on your current income and obligations. The following worksheet explains how to compute your own debt-to-income ratio. The industry standard, as reflected in the following worksheet, is 40 percent. However, some lenders maintain higher or lower ratios.

Worksheet 6: Continued

To compute your current debt-to-income ratio:

Step 1

   Current monthly gross income   _____

x .40 industry standard for manageable debt

= Portion of monthly gross income available   = _____
     for debt payments

Step 2

Monthly rent or mortgage payment   _____

+ Monthly car payment   _____

+ Minimum monthly payment on installment loan(s)   _____

+ Minimum monthly payment on all credit cards   _____

= Total monthly payments   = _____

Step 3

   40 percent of monthly gross income (result from   _____
   Step 1)

– Total monthly payments (result from Step 2)   _____

= Available for additional monthly debt payment   = _____

Ask your lender how much your minimum monthly payment will be for the supplemental loan you are considering. If that amount is larger than the amount remaining at the end of Step 3, you *and* your lender may have reason to be concerned about your ability to manage the added debt.

Worksheet 7: Cash-Flow Worksheet for Parent Borrowers

Many parents find they must borrow to help send their children to college. But before you take out a Federal PLUS Loan, it's important to understand your cash flow and know exactly how much you can afford to repay each month.

This worksheet was prepared by the College Board to help parents calculate their monthly expenses and estimate their monthly cash on hand.

MONTHLY FAMILY EXPENSES

Housing and Maintenance

❑ Mortgage or rent payment	$ _____
❑ Electricity	_____
❑ Gas	_____
❑ Water and sewer	_____
❑ Telephone	_____
❑ Property taxes	_____
❑ Homeowner's insurance	_____
❑ Household help	_____
❑ Furniture and appliances	_____
❑ Other household items	_____
❑ Home maintenance	_____
❑ Other	_____

Family

❑ Groceries	_____
❑ School lunches	_____
❑ Clothing	_____
❑ Laundry and dry cleaning	_____
❑ Toiletries	_____
❑ Prescription drugs	_____
❑ Child care	_____
❑ Education expenses	_____
❑ Children's camp expenses	_____
❑ Children's allowance	_____
❑ Gifts	_____
❑ Medical expenses	_____
❑ Medical insurance	_____
❑ Dental expenses	_____

Subtotal Monthly Expenses	$ _____

Subtotal from Previous Column $ _____

❑ Dental insurance	_____
❑ Life insurance	_____
❑ Other	_____

Transportation

❑ Automobile payments	$ _____
❑ Gasoline	_____
❑ Auto insurance	_____
❑ Auto maintenance	_____
❑ Other	_____

Leisure

❑ Movies and theater	$ _____
❑ Cable television	_____
❑ Books/magazines/newspapers	_____
❑ Vacations	_____
❑ Restaurants	_____
❑ Club memberships	_____
❑ Other	_____

Other

❑ Installment loans	$ _____
❑ Credit card debt not accounted for above	_____
❑ Investment expenses	_____
❑ Accountant's fees	_____
❑ Attorney's fees	_____
❑ Charitable and political contributions	_____
❑ Other	_____

TOTAL Monthly Expenses	$ _____

Worksheet 7: Continued

Monthly Income

❏ Net monthly income after
 taxes and payroll deductions

$ _____

❏ Rent paid to you

_____

❏ Alimony received

_____

❏ Interest and divided income

_____

Total Monthly Income $ _____

TOTAL Monthly Income $ _____

Minus

TOTAL Monthly Expenses $ _____

Equals

**Cash on Hand After
Monthly Expenses** $ _____

NOTE: Financial planners suggest that a family's outstanding debt should not be greater than 38 to 40 percent of the family's net income.

8 $ Is It WORTH It? Maybe My Child Should Just Get a Job!

At some point in the financial aid application process, you may begin to wonder if it is all worth it. In fact, it's probably safe to say that most families reach a point of at least mild frustration as they gather information about college costs and what their expected contribution will be. It probably doesn't help to continue hearing via the media that college costs in the past decade rose well above the rate of inflation. You may wonder if your child would be better off getting a job now rather than tying up current income and assets (as well as future ones if loans will be part of how you and your child meet college costs).

While each family must develop its own priorities and determine how higher education fits into those priorities, there are some key factors to keep in mind as you make decisions about the value of a college education and the role of finances in your child's decision about where to attend college.

First, there may be some better news in terms of rising college costs. Many experts are convinced that the steep increases in college costs of the 1980s are a thing of the past. Demographics indicate that there will be a significant increase in the number of students of college-going age in the next several years, so colleges may be able to spread out their costs over more students. Colleges are aware of the media, too! The majority of colleges are working to keep their costs down lest parents send their children to less expensive institutions.

 All colleges cost too much.

Actually, very few colleges are truly high-priced. While college costs have risen higher than the inflation rate, college remains accessible and affordable for a majority of Americans. The media has focused attention on the highest priced colleges (those with tuition and fees over $30,000). The reality is that only 5 percent of full-time students enroll in four-year institutions costing more than $33,000 annually. Don't let the misinformation discourage you and your child from the pursuit of higher education!

On average, full-time students receive about $9,000 of aid per year in the form of grants and tax benefits in private four-year institutions, $3,100 in public four-year institutions, and $2,200 in private two-year colleges. (From *Trends in College Pricing, 2006*.)

Another way to evaluate college costs and long-term benefits is by examining earnings premiums of college graduates over time. By the age of 33, the typical college graduate who enrolled at age 18 has earned enough to compensate for both tuition and fees at the average public four-year institution and earnings forgone during the college years. (See graph on page 97.)

Estimated Cumulative Earnings Net of College Costs

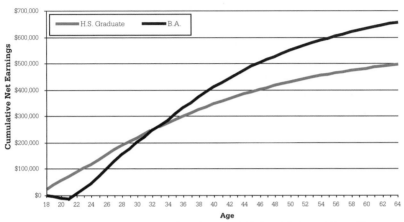

(From *Education Pays: The Benefits of Higher Education for Individuals and Society, 2004*, p. 12)*

Why do colleges cost what they do?

Each college has its own answer to this question—but there are some common factors that are helpful to understand.

Colleges Are People Oriented

It's really not possible—or desirable—to make the process of education run like a factory. As you know from your own experience, every student is different, and the teachers who make the most difference in your child's life are the ones who take the time to connect. Highly educated and skilled professors are not an inexpensive commodity, especially in fields like the sciences and engineering, where industry can offer high salaries to draw teachers away. Faculty salaries are a major factor in college costs.

Maintenance and Energy Costs

Consider the costs of maintaining your family dwelling, and multiply exponentially to get some idea of what colleges face. Estimates are staggering for what it will cost to repair and bring into the twenty-first century thousands of campus buildings that were built decades ago. From a cost perspective, consider the energy costs of everything from minifridges to computer workstations, multiplied by the hundreds or thousands of students and faculty using them on campus.

*For more information, visit http://www.collegeboard.com/research/home.

Technology

Colleges need to cover the costs of providing computer hardware and the networks and mainframes to support them. And then there are the employees who must support the computers and the student and faculty users. In the sciences, there are the additional costs of providing leading-edge research instruments and laboratories. In the arts, even "old technology" can be expensive, given the costs of providing metalworking, enameling, firing, and other specialized facilities.

Declining State Support

Unless your home state enjoys a very high and stable financial base, lawmakers must perform a balancing act every year. State appropriations to education are often an area where cuts are made, or at least increases are not approved. Public colleges depend on the states for the majority of their finances. When budget requests are not approved, tuition increases for in-state and out-of-state students may become a major source of revenue.

Family and Student Expectations

This is not to blame the victim, but it is true that many of the costs associated with higher education have to do with the cocurricular aspects of a college education. For example, students and parents expect top-notch athletic, recreational, and cultural facilities, as well as attractive grounds, varied food service, modern student health facilities, and career placement offices with online databases and staff to provide interview and résumé counseling. Colleges must spend money to upgrade their facilities to attract students to their campuses.

Is Cost the Only Issue?

If you are certain you will need financial aid to send your child to college, then it would be foolish to suggest that he or she apply only to high-cost institutions or those offering little financial assistance. In fact, every family should consider having at least one "economically safe" college on the list: one where the costs are low and/or the chances for receiving aid, given your child's qualifications, are high. But even this economically safe option should be one your child would be happy to attend if it were the only viable option at the end of the process.

In getting caught up in the financial implications, parents sometimes lose sight of the other factors that might make a particular college a good choice for their child. You don't want your child to end up at a college your family can easily afford but where he or she is unhappy, unchallenged, or unable to pursue a chosen academic major. Many admissions officers use the term "fit" to describe the relationship between a student and what a college has to offer. Some of the factors to consider in determining which colleges would be a good "fit" for your child are:

Size

Some students are happiest at smaller colleges where they can get to know most of the other students and the faculty. Others thrive on the variety and energy of a very large university.

Location

Some students will only be happy if they stay close to home, others only if they put some distance between themselves and their home. Some prefer the opportunities afforded by an urban area; others find the bucolic setting of a small-town college more appealing.

Curriculum

It's important to be sure that your child can pursue the major she or he has settled on at this stage—and that there are other options if she or he is like the majority of students who change their major while they are in college.

Other Students

Your child will probably be most comfortable in a setting where he or she is not at the very bottom of the class—or where his or her abilities far outshine those of the majority of students. If your child has special cocurricular interests (sailing, mountain climbing), he or she will be happier in a setting that attracts other students with the same interests.

Job Placement

How likely is the college to support your child in the job search? How successful have alumni been in securing good positions in fields that interest your child?

Graduate School Placement

How likely is the college to prepare your child for graduate school and support his or her application for further study? What percentage of students go on for further study?

You and your child probably considered all or most of these aspects, as well as others, when putting together the college list, but sometimes these important factors are obscured when the financial realities set in. Be sure to keep them in mind when making the final decision about where (or even if) your child attends college.

Data continue to support the assumption that the more advanced the education, the higher the expected lifetime earnings. According to recent data from *Education Pays: The Benefits of Higher Education for Individuals and Society,** people with bachelor's degrees earn about 62 percent more in a lifetime than their counterparts with only high school degrees. More educated people are also less likely to be unemployed and less likely to rely on government assistance programs.

Nonmonetary benefits from college—those that contribute to both the individual's and to society's well-being—are also significant. For example:

➡ The incarceration rate of adults with some college education is about one-quarter of that for high school graduates.

➡ College graduates take better care of their health than do high school graduates, according to the National Center for Health Statistics data. For example, only half as many smoke cigarettes and more than a third exercise regularly.

➡ Children of college graduates have higher cognitive skill levels and evidence greater ability to persist at tasks than children of mothers with lower levels of education.

➡ According to the U.S. Census Bureau, in the 2004 presidential election, 76 percent of citizens with college degrees between the ages of 25 and 44 voted, compared to 45 percent of high school graduates.

By pulling together all of the evidence about the benefits of higher education, you may find that it is worth the financial strength—or sacrifice—to ensure that your child finds a comfortable environment where he or she will thrive. In the long term, it will be better to have a happy and fulfilled child than a happy and fulfilled checkbook.

*To review the complete publication, visit http://www.collegeboard.com/research/home.

One place to begin your college selection process is at www.collegeboard.com/myroad. This unique self-assessment service allows students to explore career interests, majors, and college options in a personalized and dynamic Web-based environment. MyRoad™ facilitates the college search process by providing an online assessment of the student's interests and then linking those assessment results to career choices, major choices, and school choices. In addition, students can choose to share their progress with their school counselors by having their visits to MyRoad sent electronically to the "Counselor's Corner," which is linked to the high school.

Where Sarah, James, and Maria Have Decided to Go and Why

Sarah Smith

Sarah has decided to attend Central, based on qualitative and quantitative considerations. While Old Bricks and Central, her top two choices, both have excellent English programs, Central also has an option to prepare for a career in teaching, should she choose that path. Central's location in a small town is appealing to Sarah as a change from city life. Sarah also prefers to take on less debt her first year in college.

James Washington

James has decided to enroll at Very Old Bricks, because the grant level in his aid package made it a very affordable choice. At Very Old Bricks, he will have access to the latest in technology as he prepares for a career in engineering. The college's record in placing students in excellent first jobs and in leading graduate programs also influenced his decision. The campus spirit he felt and the types of students he met when he visited convinced him that Very Old Bricks was the place for him.

Maria Martinez

Given the fact that she's preparing to face high medical school costs after she completes her undergraduate degree, Maria has decided to attend Canyon for the first two years and then transfer to a four-year institution to complete her bachelor's degree. She has checked the medical school admissions statistics for students who transfer from Canyon to a four-year institution and is convinced that her decision will not impact negatively her chances of being admitted to a top medical school, assuming she keeps up her excellent academic record. Her parents have taken out a home equity line of credit to spread out the costs over the academic year. Maria has arranged for on-campus employment in a research lab, where she can earn money and gain experience for medical school. She is excited about the college opportunities that await her at Canyon.

 For more information about college choice:

www.collegeboard.com/myroad

College admissions offices

College alumni and current students

College and university Web sites

High school counselors

9 How Does the High School Student Fit into the Partnership?

The preceding chapters have been addressed to your parents, who will probably take the lead in making sure you have the resources you need to attend college. These final two chapters are devoted to you, the student, because you should be aware of specific ways you can participate in the financing of your own education, both while you are still in high school and later as a college student.

What You Can Do While You Are Still in High School

Ask Questions

Arrange your college visits to allow time to meet with admissions and financial aid counselors who can help you and your family answer the "Questions Families Should Ask" presented throughout this book.

Keep Track of Deadlines

Take responsibility for gathering the necessary financial aid application forms and work with your parents to be sure that forms are completed accurately and submitted by the deadlines. Refer often to the worksheet in Chapter 5 to be sure you are taking the right steps at the right time.

Be Ready to Help Financially

Prepare to contribute what is expected of you by the colleges to which you apply. A percentage of your assets, if you have any, will be expected. Many colleges will expect you to contribute a set amount from any job earnings. Keep in mind that if you spend your savings on a car, your investment will depreciate, while your investment in higher education will appreciate!

Learn the Basics of Borrowing

When you take out your first student loan, you begin a relationship with your lender that will last for many years. That's why it's so important to get all the facts and choose your lender with care.

The fact is, not all lenders are alike. Until recently, all lenders were banks. Now, some educational associations and other organizations also offer student loans. Because these nonbank lenders are part of educational programs, they often offer some special free programs and services that are very helpful to students. Be sure to ask your financial aid administrator about these programs.

Choose the lender that's right for you. When you get down to talking with lenders, don't be afraid to ask questions. Carefully compare what each has to offer before you decide on a lender. Remember, it's your future income that's at stake.

Here are some questions you'll want to ask each lender you are considering:

➡ **How long will it take to get my loan?** The time it takes to process your application and get you your loan funds (the turnaround time) varies greatly between lenders.

Make sure you tell the lender if timing is important to you.

Do you sell your student loans? Many lenders sell their loans to other lenders or to a secondary market. The secondary market is made up of many private and state-run organizations that specialize in buying student loans. Although there is nothing wrong with this practice, it can be confusing to students. Each time your loan is sold, you will be dealing with a new owner and their policies, and not the people who gave you the loan. But rest assured, the interest rate and terms of your loan will not change.

To avoid confusion, choose a lender that sells to only one secondary market—and use that lender for all your student loans. That way, all your loans will be in the same place.

Do you use a servicer? Some lenders and all secondary markets have contracts with student loan servicers. These companies take care of all the details—like originating the loan, collecting and processing payments, handling questions from students, and maintaining the loan records—and generally "service" your loan account. If your lender uses a servicer, you will communicate with the servicer, and not the lender, for questions about your loan or changes in your address or student status. Many services offer online account access to your loan records.

Do you capitalize interest payments? Most lenders allow you to delay making interest payments (if due) until you begin repaying your loan. With capitalization, accrued interest is added to your principal (the amount you borrow) on your unsubsidized Federal Stafford Loans. This increases your balance (the amount you owe) and your monthly payments. A lender may capitalize your interest every three months; every six months; once each year; or just one time, when repayment begins. (It's the lender's choice.)

To save big money, choose a lender that offers one-time capitalization at repayment.

➡ **What types of repayment assistance plans do you offer?** Choose a lender that offers repayment options such as graduated repayment and loan consolidation.

> With graduated repayment, your monthly loan payments start at a lower amount when your income is lower and gradually increase as your income grows.

> Loan consolidation allows you to combine all your student loans into one monthly payment. This lowers the amount of each payment but increases the length of the repayment period. Sometimes your interest rate will increase, as well. Ask the lender to show you how consolidation works.

➡ **What is your forbearance (hardship) policy?** Some lenders will be willing to let you defer your loan payments for a time if you run into trouble repaying your loan. Choose a lender with a flexible forbearance policy.

➡ **Will you be easy to contact?** The last thing you need is a lender who puts you on hold when you call. Choose a lender with student-friendly services like toll-free telephone numbers, and a helpful staff that answers your questions and provides guidance when you call.

Remember: You are the customer. Plenty of lenders want your business. Choose the lender who will do the best job for you.

Finish High School on a High Note

You'll face lots of distractions as you wind up your high school career: co-curricular and social activities, the whole admissions and financial aid application process, and other obligations. In the midst of all this, don't forget to keep up with your academics. Not only will a strong high school record enable you to hit the ground running when you start college, but it may help you qualify for the type of financial aid colleges award to their preferred candidates. So keep up the good work!

 For more information on student financing options:

College admissions and financial aid offices

College and university Web sites

College Board on the Web: www.collegeboard.com

Guide to Getting Financial Aid 2008

High school counselors

Need a Lift? Educational Opportunities, Careers, Loans, Scholarships, Employment, 46th ed. (Indianapolis: The American Legion Education Program). Updated annually. Sources of career, scholarship, and loan information for all students, with emphasis on scholarships for veterans, their dependents, and children of deceased or disabled veterans.

The Student Guide (Washington, D.C.: U.S. Department of Education, Office of Student Financial Assistance). Detailed information on federal student aid programs, eligibility rules, application procedures. Free. Order from Federal Student Aid Programs by calling 800 433-3243.

10 How Does the College Student Fit into the Partnership?

Once you are in college, you'll have plenty to keep you busy, academically and socially. The challenges of applying for admission and first-year financial aid will be replaced by new challenges. Yet you'll want to keep on top of your finances throughout college, not only to ensure that you can continue to pay for college but also to ensure that you begin your postcollege years on as firm a financial footing as possible.

Managing Your Money Responsibly
Develop a Budget

A simple budget plan will help you avoid problems like running out of money before the semester is over. Write down all your financial obligations in one column and the funds or income that will cover those obligations in another. Think about the way you'll spend your money each month during the school year. Then, write out your budget plan, consult it often, and stick to it! The worksheet at the end of this chapter will help you get started.

Open a Checking Account

A checking account will help you keep track of where your money goes. Always keep enough money in your checking account to cover the checks you write. Record all your deposits, withdrawals, and checks in your checkbook register; balance your checkbook every month. Hold onto your canceled checks because they provide a record of your spending and serve as proof that you paid for something.

Beware of the ATM

Many banks have automated teller machines, which can be a real convenience if you need cash after regular banking hours or when you're too busy to get to the bank. But they can also be the fast track to financial problems because it's so easy to withdraw money. Try not to visit the ATM too often. When you do make withdrawals, you'll waste less money if you take out smaller amounts. Save your ATM receipts and be sure to record them in your checkbook register. Keep your ATM card in a secure place.

Say "No" to Credit Cards

Credit cards are a great way to get into financial trouble. Banks are happy to offer you a credit card; but beware, these cards are really loans in disguise because the bank charges you interest if you don't pay the whole bill at the end of the month. When you use your credit card, you must make a monthly payment that includes interest or finance charges of up to 20 percent until the total bill is paid off. You may also have to pay an annual fee just for use of the card. You could pay even more if you use your card to get a cash advance (a very bad idea). If you feel you must have a credit card, save it for a real money emergency.

Pay Bills on Time

If you can't pay the whole amount you owe, pay the minimum allowed on the bill. By making at least the minimum payment each month, you'll have a clean payment record and build a good credit rating for the future.

Reduce Your Costs

Write letters or send e-mail instead of calling long distance. Buy used books instead of new ones, or pool resources with friends and share books. Save more money by reading library copies of some of the books on your list. Compare residence hall costs with those of apartment living. Some students can save substantial amounts by living off campus and sharing the costs of rent and utilities. (Of course, this works only if you avoid high-rent districts and find good roommates.) Or you may be in a situation where continuing to live at home makes sense. No matter where you live, you can make your money go further by fixing some of your own meals and taking advantage of free campus entertainment.

Accelerate Your Degree

This isn't an option for everyone, but if you come into college with some credits earned in high school, or take college courses in the summer, you may be able to graduate a semester or more early, thus saving tuition and living expenses.

Financial Aid Renewal

Keep Your Grades Up

Many grant and loan programs, including those administered through the federal government, require that you maintain a certain grade point average (GPA) and make satisfactory progress toward a degree in order to qualify for renewal of aid.

Learn Your College's Renewal Policies

If you haven't already checked with your college's financial aid office about their aid renewal policies, be sure to do so in the first semester. You'll want to be sure to have the required forms on hand.

Be Timely and Accurate When You Renew Your Application

Be aware of the deadlines for applying for aid renewal, and work with your parents to be sure forms are completed accurately and submitted on time.

Borrow Responsibly

Borrow only what you need. Being eligible to borrow doesn't mean you have to take the maximum the lender will allow. Remember, you're expected to repay your loans, plus interest. Repaying your loans on time will help you establish a good credit rating—very important when it's time to find a job, rent an apartment, or buy a car.

Education Loan Pop Quiz

You probably won't find a course in your college's catalog called Education Loan 101. Regardless, what you know about your loans has a profound, long-term impact on your financial life. Here's a pop quiz of 10 questions to help you assess what you know about your education loans. The answers apply to most loan programs. Some refer specifically to education loans that are sponsored by the College Board.

1. You can apply for a Stafford Loan only if you're a full-time undergraduate student.
   ☐ True
   ☐ False

2. Defaulting on education loans will not adversely affect you since your lender can't "repossess" your education
   ☐ True
   ☐ False

3. Your lender will try to find a way to make loan repayment easier if you're running into trouble.
   ☐ True
   ☐ False

4. There's no way to reduce the amount of your student loan except through actual repayment.
   ☐ True
   ☐ False

5. Not all education loans are need based.
   ☐ True
   ☐ False

6. There are several types of repayment options.
   ☐ True
   ☐ False

7. Your new address is automatically sent to your loan servicer when you move or transfer to a different institution.
   ☐ True
   ☐ False

8. You don't have to pay back your education loans if you don't graduate.
   ☐ True
   ☐ False

9. Late or missed education loan repayments don't affect your personal credit.
   ☐ True
   ☐ False

10. Timely education loan repayment can help you establish good credit.
    ☐ True
    ☐ False

Answers

1. **False.** Undergraduate and graduate students enrolled at least half-time in a degree or certificate program are eligible to apply for both subsidized and unsubsidized Stafford Loans.

2. **False.** If you don't pay back your loans, the IRS can go after your income tax refunds, garnish your wages, and collect fees—plus your credit history goes down the tubes.

3. **True.** Most lenders will lower your loan payments or defer them for a time.

4. **False.** Many lenders offer special borrower benefit programs (interest rate reductions, principal rebates, "cash back," etc.) based on good repayment behavior.

5. **True.** Many loans are not need based. These loans include unsubsidized Stafford Loans and PLUS Loans.

6. **True.** In addition to standard repayment, you can generally choose from graduated and income-sensitive repayment options.

7. **False.** You must notify your lender of your new address immediately.

8. **False.** You have to pay back your loans whether or not you graduate.

9. **False.** A bad education loan repayment history is a sure path to bad credit.

10. **True.** If you show that you can pay back your education loans as scheduled, you're also proving you are creditworthy.

Results

10: Move to the head of the class.

8 to 9: A solid B with this caveat—what you don't know can hurt you.

5 to 7: Time to read over material from your financial aid office.

0 to 4: Yikes! Make an appointment with your financial aid adviser now.

Your Credit History and Professional School

If you're planning to apply for admission to professional school, it's likely you'll need to borrow money to continue your education. But did you know that your admission may be dependent on your ability to demonstrate clean credit? You'll need a credit history, in the form of a credit report, that shows you've been responsible in paying back your debts.

Most professional schools will require a copy of your credit report after you've been accepted for admission but before you've been offered a financial aid package. If your credit report shows a number of late or missed payments on your credit cards or car loan, for example, or charging over your credit limit, you could be denied admission or an alternative loan for graduate school.

The following are answers to questions regarding credit reports and how to get a negative credit history back on track without jeopardizing your education.

When should I get a copy of my credit report?

Send for it well before you apply to graduate or professional school. This will give you time to review your credit history and resolve problems or errors you may find in your report. Ask your financial aid office which credit reporting agency they use, then contact that agency to request a copy of your report. There are three major reporting agencies—Experian, TransUnion, and Equifax—and each could have its own file on you. If you want to review your credit history, you may call TransUnion at 800 888-4213 for recorded instructions. If they do not have a file on you, call Experian at 888 397-3742, and then Equifax at 800 685-1111. If you would like to obtain your report online, go to www.experian.com, www.transunion.com, www.equifax.com, or www.creditreport-net.com. You will be able to print the report from the Web site. The fee will be charged to your credit card.

What should I do when I receive my credit report?

Check the report carefully for errors. Make sure the reporting agency hasn't confused you with someone else with the same name or a similar social security number, and that they haven't included incorrect information about you and your accounts. If you find a mistake or have questions about your report, follow the instructions included in the report. If you do not receive a reply within 30 days, call the credit reporting agency.

What if I disagree with information in my credit report?

For those items in your credit report that you disagree with, such as a credit card account that was paid late due to unexpected medical bills or another real financial emergency, send a brief statement to the credit reporting agency. The information you provide will be placed on your credit profile and will be included each time your report is accessed.

What if my credit report shows one or more 90-day delinquencies or my school or lender determines I have a negative credit history?

You may still be able to borrow if you can document extenuating circumstances. Your documentation may include, but is not limited to:

➡ An updated credit report that shows you are no longer 90 or more days delinquent on a debt. You may also use an updated report to correct other information on the original credit report that resulted in the adverse ruling.

➡ A statement from your creditors that you have made satisfactory arrangements to repay the debt or debts that are the basis for the adverse credit ruling.

➡ In the case of a debt with an outstanding balance that is less than $500 but is 90 or more days delinquent, you may provide, in writing, a satisfactory explanation for the delinquency.

I have late payments on my credit report, and I don't want potential lenders or employers to see them. Should I use one of those companies that claim they can get this kind of information removed from my credit report?

No. Companies that say they can "fix" your credit profile are usually scams that take your money. There is nothing they can do for you that you cannot do for yourself. Accurate information remains part of your credit history, whether positive or not. Only time will fix bad credit.

How long does negative credit information remain in my file?

Credit and collection accounts and court records, such as judgments, remain on file for seven years (five years in New York) from the date of last activity. It's important to remember that even if you paid your account in full, the negative information will not be removed from your credit file until the required number of years have passed. However, the account will appear as paid on your report.

Can I rebuild my credit history?

Yes. The good news is, your credit report is continually evolving. When you use credit responsibly and pay your bills on time, you're building a positive credit history. When a lender or credit card issuer considers your application, it often pays much more attention to your bill-paying pattern during the most recent two years than to your record of five years ago or longer. The negative information on your report should not prevent you from borrowing in the future if you can demonstrate that you are a good credit risk by paying your bills on time over a period of 18 to 24 months.

Where can I get help in managing my debts?

If you're finding it difficult to pay your bills, the nonprofit National Foundation for Consumer Credit has member agencies that can help you establish a budget and negotiate a repayment plan with your creditors. Call 800 388-2227 for the location of an agency near you. Credit counseling is also available online at www.nfcc.org.

 For more information on responsible student financing:

College financial aid office

College Web site

College Board on the Web: www.collegeboard.com

 Questions Students Should Ask the College About the Financial Aid Reapplication Process

1. What financial aid forms are required for aid renewal?

2. When are the forms due to be completed and returned to the processor and/or college?

3. Will renewal of financial aid be dependent on my academic progress? What are the guidelines for maintaining satisfactory academic progress?

4. Will a copy of my parents' completed tax forms be required? If so, when?

5. When will I receive notification of my financial aid package?

6. What is the deadline for accepting the financial aid offer?

Worksheet 8: Budgeting for the Semester

Estimated Expenses for Semester

Tuition	$ _____
Fees	_____
Books/Supplies	_____
Rent/Housing	_____
Board/Meals	_____
Phone/Utilities	_____
Clothing	_____
Laundry/Dry Cleaning	_____
Transportation (carfare, gas, parking, insurance, etc.)	_____
Medical/Dental	_____
Recreation	_____
Personal Expenses	_____
Savings	_____
Child Care	_____
Credit Card Debt	_____
Other	_____
TOTAL SEMESTER EXPENSES	$ _____

Projected Income for Semester

Money from Parents	$ _____
Money from Savings	_____
Work-Study	_____
Other Work	_____
Scholarships	_____
Grants	_____
Loans	_____
Public Benefits (Social Security, Veterans Admin., etc.)	_____
Spouse's Wages	_____
Other	_____
TOTAL SEMESTER INCOME	$ _____

NOTE: If your total semester expenses exceed your total semester income, carefully review your spending habits and look for areas where you can economize.

Worksheet 9: Tracking Financial Aid Renewal Requirements

Use this worksheet to keep track of deadlines for renewing your financial aid award. Your financial aid administrator will provide you with renewal requirements.

Forms	Required?	Due Date	Date Completed
Renewal FAFSA			
CSS/Financial Aid PROFILE			
• Registration			
• Application			
College Application			
Tax Forms			
Other:			

Appendix

A State-by-State Summary of College Savings and Prepaid Tuition Plans		
State	Program Name and Contact Information	Plan Type
AK	**University of Alaska College Savings Plan** University of Alaska 866 277-1005 http://www.uacollegesavings.com	Savings
	or **T. Rowe Price** https: www.price529.com	Savings
	John Hancock Freedom 529 866 222-7498 http://www.johnhancockfreedom529.com	Savings
AL	**Prepaid Affordable Tuition Plan (PACT)** State Treasurer 800 252-7228	Prepaid
	or **Van Kampen Investments** 866 529-2228 http://www.treasury.state.al.us	Savings
AZ	**Arizona Family College Savings Programs (AFCSP)** http://arizona.collegesavings.com	Savings
	or **Fidelity Arizona College Savings Plan** Fidelity Investments 800 544-1262 http://personal.fidelity.com/planning/investment	Savings

	Waddell & Reed InvestEd Plan 888 923-3355 http://www.waddell.com	Savings
AR	**GIFT College Investing Plan** Franklin Templeton Investments/Mercury Advisors 800 587-7301 http://thegiftplan.uii.upromise.com	Savings
CA	**The ScholarShare College Savings Plan** Golden State ScholarShare 800 544-5248 http://www.scholarshare.com	Savings
	Scholar Share Advisor College Savings Plan http://www.advisor.fidelity.com	Savings
CO	**Scholars Choice College Savings Program** Scholars Choice 888 572-4652 http://www.collegeinvest.org or http://www.scholars-choice.com	Savings
	Direct Porfolio College Savings Plan 800 448-2424 http://www.collegeinvest.org	Savings
	Stable Value Plus College Savings Program 800 448-2424 www.collegeinvest.org	Savings
CT	**Connecticut Higher Education Trust (CHET)** Connecticut's 529 College Savings Program 888 799-2438 http://www.aboutchet.com	Savings
DC	**DC529 College Savings Program** 800 987-4859 http://www.dccollegesavings.com	Savings
DE	**Delaware College Investment Plan** 800 544-1655 http://personal.fidelity.com/planning/investment	Savings
FL	**Florida Prepaid College Plan** Florida Prepaid College Program Board 800 552-4723 http://www.florida529plans.com	Prepaid
	or **Florida College Investment Plan** Florida Prepaid College Program Board 800 552-4723 http://www.florida529plans.com	Savings
GA	**Georgia Higher Education Savings Plan** 877 424-4377 http://www.gacollegesavings.com	Savings
HI	**TuitionEDGE** Delaware Investments TuitionEDGE Plan 866 529-3343	Savings
IA	**College Savings Iowa** Iowa State Treasurer's Office 888 672-9116 http://collegesavingsiowa.uii.upromise.com	Savings

	Iowa Advisor 529 Plan 800 774-5127 http://iowaadvisor592.uii.upromise.com	Savings
ID	**Idaho College Savings Program (IDeal)** 866 433-2533 http://www.idsaves.org	Savings
IL	**College Illinois! 529 Prepaid Tuition Plan** 877 877-3724 http://www.collegeillinois.com	Prepaid
	or **Bright Start College Savings Program** 877 432-7444 http://www.brightstartsavings.com	Savings
	Bright Directions College Savings Program 866 722-7283 http://www.brightdirections.com	Savings
IN	**CollegeChoice 529 Investment Plan** One Group Investments 866 400-7526 http://www.collegechoiceplan.com	Savings
KS	**Learning Quest 529 Education Savings Program** American Century 800 579-2203 https://www.learningquestsavings.com	Savings
	or **Schwab 529 College Savings Plan** 888 903-3863 http://www.schwab.com	Savings
	Learning Quest Advisor 877 882-6236 http://www.learningquestsavings.com	
KY	**Kentucky's Affordable Prepaid Tuition (KAPT)** Kentucky Higher Education Assistance Authority 888 919-5278 http://www.getkapt.com	Prepaid
	or **Kentucky Education Savings Plan Trust** Kentucky Higher Education Assistance Authority 877 598-7878 http://www.kysaves.com	Savings
LA	**START Saving Program** Louisiana Office of Student Financial Assistance 800 259-5626 http://www.startsaving.la.gov/savings	Savings
MA	**The U.Plan** Massachusetts Educational Finance Authority 800 449-6332 http://www.mefa.org	Prepaid

	or **The U.Fund College Investing Plan** Massachusetts Educational Finance Authority and Fidelity Investments 800 544-2776 http://personal.fidelity.com/planning/investment	Savings
MD	**Prepaid College Trust** College Savings Plans of Maryland 888 463-4723 http://www.collegesavingsmd.org	Prepaid
	or **College Investment Plan** College Savings Plans of Maryland 888 463-4723 http://www.collegesavingsmd.org	Savings
ME	**NextGen College Investing Plan** Merrill Lynch 877 463-9843 http://www.nextgenplan.com	Savings
MI	**Michigan Education Trust (MET)** Michigan Department of Treasury 800 638-4543 http://www.michigan.gov/treasury	Prepaid
	or **Michigan Education Savings Program (MESP)** Michigan Department of Treasury 877 861-6377 http://www.misaves.com	Savings
MN	**Minnesota College Savings Plan** 877 338-4646 http://www.mnsaves.org	Savings
MO	**Missouri 529 College Savings Plan (MOST)** 888 414-6678 https://www.missourimost.s.upromise.com	Savings
	MOST-Missouri's 529 Advisor Plan 800 617-5097 http://most529advisor.uii.upromise.com/individual/	Savings
MS	**Mississippi Prepaid Affordable College Tuition Program (MPACT)** Mississippi State Treasury Department 800 987-4450 http://www.collegesavingsmississippi.com	Prepaid
	or **Mississippi Affordable College Savings (MACS)** 800 486-3670 http://www.collegesavingsms.com	Savings
	MACS 529 Advisor Program 877 238-7529 http://www.529advisorprograms.com	Savings
MT	**Montana Family Education Savings Program** 800 888-2723 http://montana.collegesavings.com	Savings
	or **CollegeSure 529** Montana Commission for Higher Education 800 888-2723 http://montana.collegesavings.com	Savings

	Pacific Life Funds 529 College Savings Plan 800 722-2333 (Advisor-Sold) & http://www.pacificlife.com (Direct-Sold)	Savings
NC	**North Carolina's National College Savings Program** College Foundation of North Carolina 800 600-3453 http://www.cfnc.org/savings	Savings
ND	**College Save** 866 728-3529 http://www.collegesave4U.com	Savings
NE	**College Savings Plan of Nebraska** Nebraska State Treasurer 888 993-3746 (Advisor-Sold) & http://www.planforcollegenow.com (Direct-Sold)	Savings
	or **TD Ameritrade 529 College Savings Plan** 877 408-4644 http://www.collegesavings.tdameritrade.com	Savings
	AIM College Savings Plan 877 246-7526 http://www.aiminvestments.com	Savings
	State Farm College Savings Plan 800 321-7520 http://statefarm.com/mutual/acct_types/529.asp	Savings
NH	**UNIQUE College Investing Plan** Fidelity Investments 800 544-1722 http://personal.fidelity.com/planning	Savings
	Fidelity Advisor 529 Plan 800 522-7297 http://advisorfidelity.com	Savings
NJ	**New Jersey Better Educational Savings Trust (NJBEST)** Higher Education Student Assistance Authority 877 465-2378 http://www.njbest.com	Savings
	Franklin Templeton 529 College Savings Plan 866 362-1597 www.franklintempleton.com	Savings
NM	**The Education Plan** The Education Plan of New Mexico 877 337-5268 http://www.theeducationplan.com	Savings
	College Sense 529 Higher Education Savings Plan 866 529-7367 http://www.collegesense.com	Savings

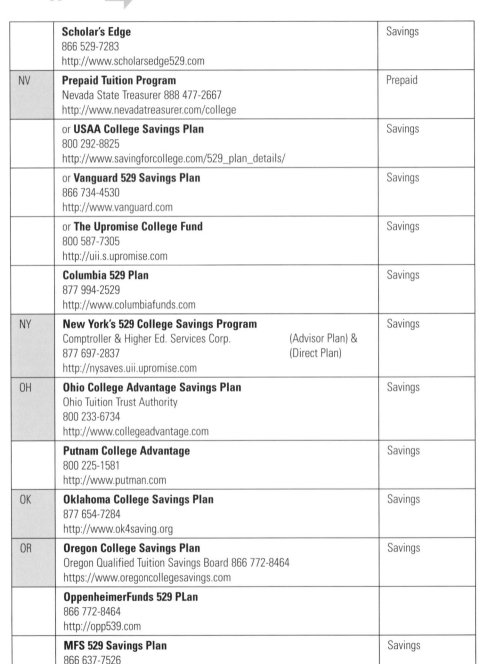

	Scholar's Edge 866 529-7283 http://www.scholarsedge529.com	Savings
NV	**Prepaid Tuition Program** Nevada State Treasurer 888 477-2667 http://www.nevadatreasurer.com/college	Prepaid
	or **USAA College Savings Plan** 800 292-8825 http://www.savingforcollege.com/529_plan_details/	Savings
	or **Vanguard 529 Savings Plan** 866 734-4530 http://www.vanguard.com	Savings
	or **The Upromise College Fund** 800 587-7305 http://uii.s.upromise.com	Savings
	Columbia 529 Plan 877 994-2529 http://www.columbiafunds.com	Savings
NY	**New York's 529 College Savings Program** Comptroller & Higher Ed. Services Corp. (Advisor Plan) & 877 697-2837 (Direct Plan) http://nysaves.uii.upromise.com	Savings
OH	**Ohio College Advantage Savings Plan** Ohio Tuition Trust Authority 800 233-6734 http://www.collegeadvantage.com	Savings
	Putnam College Advantage 800 225-1581 http://www.putman.com	Savings
OK	**Oklahoma College Savings Plan** 877 654-7284 http://www.ok4saving.org	Savings
OR	**Oregon College Savings Plan** Oregon Qualified Tuition Savings Board 866 772-8464 https://www.oregoncollegesavings.com	Savings
	OppenheimerFunds 529 PLan 866 772-8464 http://opp539.com	
	MFS 529 Savings Plan 866 637-7526 http://www.mfs.com	Savings

PA	**Tuition Account Program (TAP 529) – Guaranteed Savings Plan** Pennsylvania State Treasury 800 440-4000 http://www.tap529.com	Guaranteed Savings
	or **Pennsylvannia 529 Direct Investment Plan** 800 294-6195 www.pa529direct.com	Savings
RI	**College Bound Fund** AllianceBernstein (Advisor-Sold) & 888 324-5057 (Direct-Sold) http://ri.collegeboundfund.com	Savings
SC	**South Carolina Tuition Prepayment Program (SCTPP)** South Carolina Office of State Treasurer 888 772-4723 http://www.scgrad.org	Prepaid
	or **FUTURE Scholar** Nations Funds 888 244-5674 (Advisor-Sold) & http://www.futurescholar.com (Direct-Sold)	Savings
SD	**College Access 529** Pimco Funds 866 529-7462 (Advisor-Sold) & http://www.collegeaccess529.com (Direct-Sold)	Savings
TN	**BEST Prepaid College Tuition Plan** 888 486-2378 http://treasury.state.tn.us/best	Prepaid
	or **BEST Savings Plan** State of Tennessee Treasury Department 888 486-2378 http://www.tnbest.org	Savings
TX	**Tomorrow's College Investment Plan** Texas Comptroller of Public Accounts 800 445-4723 (Advisor-Sold) & http://www.enterprise529.com (Direct-Sold)	Savings
UT	**Utah Educational Savings Plan Trust (UESP)** Utah State Board of Regents 800 418-2551 http://www.uesp.org	Savings
VA	**Virginia Prepaid Education Program (VPEP)** Virginia College Savings Plan 888 567-0540 http://www.virginia529.com	Prepaid
	or **Virginia Education Savings Trust (VEST)** Virginia College Savings Plan 888 567-0540 http://www.virginia529.com	Savings
	College America 800 421-4120 http://www.americafunds.com	Savings

VT	**Vermont Higher Education Investment Plan** Vermont Student Assistance Corporation 800 637-5860 http://services.vsac.org	Savings
WA	**Guaranteed Education Tuition (GET) Program** Committee on Advanced Tuition Payment 877 438-8848 http://www.get.wa.gov	Prepaid
WI	**EdVest** EdVest College Savings Program 888 338-3789 (Advisor-Sold) & http://www.wellsfargoadvantagefunds.com (Direct-Sold)	Savings
	Tomorrow's Scholar 866 677-6933 http://www.wellsfargoadvantagefunds.com/wfweb/wf/scholar/index.jsp	Savings
WV	**SMART529—Direct College Savings Plan** Hartford Life Insurance Co. 866 574-3542 http://www.smart529.com	Savings
	or **SMART529 Select** 866 574-3542 www.smart529select.com	Savings
	Cournerstone SMART529 866 574-3542 http://www.smart529.com	Savings
	Director SMART529 College Savings Plan 866 574-3542 http://www.smart529.com	Savings
	Leaders SMART529 866 574-3542 http://www.smart529.com	Savings
WY	**Direct Portfolio College Savings Plan WY** 800 448-2424 http://collegeinvestwyoming.org	Savings

Glossary

Academic Competitiveness Grant: A federal grant available to Pell-eligible U.S. citizens who have completed a qualifying high school curriculum and who are enrolled full-time in a degree-granting institution. More information may be found at http://studentaid.ed.gov/PORTALSWebApp/students/english/NewPrograms.jsp.

Billable Costs: Those costs that are billed directly by the institution to the family. Billable costs include tuition and fees, as well as room and board for students living in campus housing and taking meals on campus. Billable costs are sometimes referred to as *direct* costs.

Candidate's Reply Date Agreement: Colleges adhering to this agreement will not require admitted freshman applicants to notify the college of their decision to attend, or to accept an offer of financial aid, before May 1. The purpose of the agreement is to give applicants time to hear from all the colleges to which they applied before having to make a commitment to any one of them.

Capitalization: When a lender accrues interest before the borrower begins repayment, then adds that amount to the principal. Sometimes also called "compounding." Capitalizing increases the total to be repaid and the size of the minimum monthly payment. Students can avoid capitalizing interest by paying the accrued interest. Lenders may capitalize no more frequently than quarterly; the more frequently interest is capitalized, the higher the interest payments.

Consolidation: Combining two or more loans into one new loan that has a longer repayment term and a single monthly payment that is smaller than the sum of previous monthly payments. By consolidating eligible federal student loans and extending the repayment term (up to 30 years, depending on the total loan amount), repayment can be easier. Note that while this may ease the borrower's cash flow, consolidation can add significantly to the amount of overall interest that is paid over time.

Cooperative Education: Also called "co-op education," this is a program in which students alternate between periods of full-time study and full-time paid employment, usually in a related field. Typically five years are required to complete a bachelor's degree in a cooperative education program. Some colleges refer to this as "work-study," but it should not be confused with the Federal Work-Study Program.

Cost of Attendance: This figure is determined for each college by totaling the costs for tuition and fees, room and board, books and supplies, personal expenses, and travel.

CSS/Financial Aid PROFILE®: A fully online data collection and need-analysis service required by many colleges, universities, and private scholarship programs in addition to the FAFSA. PROFILE is used in awarding private financial aid funds. Students pay a fee to register for PROFILE and have reports sent to institutions and programs that use it.

Early Decision/Early Action: These admissions programs are offered at some colleges for students who have determined that the college is their first choice. Early Decision candidates must attend the college if they are admitted under the program; Early Action candidates simply hear earlier than other students what the decision is but are not required to attend if admitted. Students may pick only one college to which to apply under an Early Decision program.

Family Contribution: The total amount a student and his or her family are expected to pay toward college costs from their income and assets. The amount is derived from a need analysis of a family's overall financial circumstances. Federal Methodology is used in determining a student's eligibility for federal, and in most cases state funded, student aid. Some colleges and private aid programs may use a different methodology (Institutional Methodology or some derivative of it) in determining eligibility for nonfederal sources of financial aid.

Federal Direct Loan Program: Students at participating colleges can borrow subsidized or unsubsidized Federal Direct Loans through this college-administered program. The federal government pays the interest on subsidized direct loans while students are enrolled in college at least half-time, if the loan is based on demonstrated need. For unsubsidized loans, students will usually be asked to make interest payments while enrolled in school. Following a six-month grace period after graduating from or leaving school, all students borrowing in the Federal Direct Loan Program must begin repaying principal and interest.

Federal Pell Grant Program: A federally sponsored and administered program that provides grants based on exceptional need to undergraduate students. Congress annually sets the dollar range for grants.

Federal Perkins Loan Program: A federally funded program based on exceptional need, administered by colleges, that provides low-interest loans for undergraduate and graduate students. Repayment does not begin until nine months after the student graduates from or leaves college.

Federal PLUS Loans: This program permits parents of dependent under-graduate students to borrow up to the full cost of education minus any other financial aid the student may have received. To be eligible, parents must usually pass a credit check.

Federal Stafford Loan Program: A federal program that allows students to borrow to meet educational expenses. Funds are borrowed directly from banks or other lending institutions. The federal government pays the interest on subsidized Stafford Loans while students are enrolled in college at least half-time, if the loan is based on demonstrated need. For unsubsidized loans, students may be asked to make interest payments while enrolled in school. Following a six-month grace period after graduating from or leaving school, all students borrowing in the Federal Stafford Loan Program must begin repaying principal and interest.

Federal Supplemental Educational Opportunity Grant (SEOG) Program: A federal program administered by colleges to provide grant aid to undergraduate students with exceptional financial need.

Federal Work-Study (FWS): A federally sponsored, campus-based program. Participating colleges provide employment opportunities for students with demonstrated need who are enrolled for undergraduate or graduate study. In assigning work to aid recipients, colleges take into account the recipient's skills, class schedule, academic progress, and interest in community service.

Financial Aid Award Letter: A notice from a college or other financial aid sponsor that tells the student how much aid is being offered. The award letter also usually explains how a student's financial need was determined, describes the contents of the financial aid package, and outlines any conditions attached to the award.

Financial Aid Package: The total financial aid award received by the student. It may be made up of a combination or "package" of aid that includes both gift aid and self-help. Many colleges try to meet a student's full financial need, but availability of funds, institutional aid policies, and the number of students needing assistance all influence the composition of a financial aid package.

Financial Need: The amount by which a student's family contribution falls short of covering the cost of attendance. Assessments of need may differ depending on the need-analysis methodology used.

Forbearance: An authorized period of time during which the lender agrees to temporarily postpone a borrower's total loan repayment obligation. At the borrower's request, an extension of time or smaller monthly payments may be authorized. Forbearance is granted at the lender's discretion when a borrower demonstrates good intentions of repaying but is temporarily unable to do so. A borrower must request forbearance from the lender. Forbearance does not alter the repayment status of the loan and interest continues to accrue.

Free Application for Federal Student Aid (FAFSA): A form distributed and processed by the United States Department of Education, used in applying for all Federal Title IV student aid programs, including Pell Grants, Stafford Loans, and campus-based programs (SEOG, Work-Study, and Perkins Loans). The FAFSA collects information required to determine eligibility according to Federal Methodology. In many states, completion of the FAFSA is also sufficient to establish eligibility for state-sponsored aid programs. Forms are widely available in high schools and colleges, and may be filed anytime after January 1 of the year for which a student is seeking aid.

Gift Aid: Student financial aid, such as scholarships and grants, that does not have to be repaid and does not require a student's being employed.

Interest: The fee charged a borrower for the use of someone else's money, computed as a percentage of what is borrowed. The interest rate may remain constant throughout the life of the loan (i.e., fixed) or may change at specified times (i.e., variable).

Lender: A financial institution such as a bank, savings and loan association, credit union, or qualified program (i.e., the College Board's Education Loan Program) that makes Federal Family Education and PLUS Loans, as well as other private loans, to students and parents.

Need Analysis: The process by which a financial aid sponsor determines a family's demonstrated need for financial assistance. Demonstrated need is determined to be the difference between what a family can afford (the family contribution) and the cost of attendance at each college to which the student applies. Differences in calculation of need arise from a variety of factors, including the methodology used to determine the family contribution and the varying costs of colleges.

Need-Blind Admissions: The policy followed by institutions that decide whether a student will be admitted without regard to the family's financial status or the amount of financial aid the student will need in order to enroll in the institution.

Need-Sensitive Admissions: The policy followed by institutions that decide whether a student will be admitted after considering the family's financial status and the amount of financial aid the student will need in order to enroll in the institution.

Noncustodial PROFILE: A fully online financial aid application system for noncustodial parents. The information contained in the application is used by institutions to determine a student's need for nonfederal institutional funds.

Parent Contribution: The amount a student's parents are expected to pay toward college costs from their income and assets. The amount is derived from a need analysis of the parents' overall financial situation. The parent contribution and the student contribution together constitute the total family contribution that, when subtracted from the cost of attendance, equals financial need. Generally, students are eligible for financial aid up to their financial need.

Satisfactory Academic Progress: Many financial aid sponsors require that students make satisfactory progress to continue to qualify for aid. To receive federal student aid, students must maintain satisfactory academic progress toward completion of a degree or certificate each term. All colleges have a statement defining the required level of progress. Some colleges have additional academic standards for renewal of institutionally sponsored awards.

Self-Help: Student financial aid, such as loans and jobs, that requires repayment or a student's being employed.

SMART Grant: (National Science and Mathematics ACCESS to RETAIN Talent Program): A federal grant program for Pell Grant recipients who are U.S. citizens. Annual grants range up to $4,000 for eligible students enrolled in qualified academic programs and who are maintaining a minimum 3.0 (on a 4.0 scale) in their major course work. More information can be found at http://studentaid.ed.gov/PORTALSWebApp/students/english/NewPrograms.jsp.

Student Aid Report (SAR): A report produced by the U.S. Department of Education and sent to students who have applied for federal financial aid. The SAR information is used by colleges to determine eligibility for Federal Pell Grants and other federal financial aid programs such as the Federal Work-Study Program, Federal Perkins Loan Program, Federal Supplemental Educational Opportunity Grants, Federal Family Education Loan Program, and the Federal Direct Loan Program.

Student Contribution: The amount students are expected to pay from their income, assets, and benefits toward college costs. The amount is derived from a need analysis of the student's resources. The student contribution and the parent contribution constitute the total family contribution that, when subtracted from the student budget, equals financial need. Generally, students are eligible for financial aid up to their financial need.

Index

About the Author

Deb Thyng Schmidt graduated from Bates College in 1977 summa cum laude and Phi Beta Kappa, and earned a master's degree in English from the University of Wisconsin-Madison in 1980. Her career has been spent in education, mainly in the area of college admissions. At Carleton College, she directed the alumni admissions volunteers program; at Cornell University, she was responsible for the development and coordination of university-wide undergraduate admissions and financial aid communications. Since moving to Colorado in 1995, she has worked as a freelance writer for a number of institutions and organizations, including the College Board, Cornell University, The Dawson School, and Marywood College. She has also served as a trustee of Bates College.